MW00612112

God's Holiness
vs. Man's Lawlessness

About the Series

Monday Blues to Sunday Pews is a grassroots series of Christian books that will lead us on a journey through each book of the Bible, one step at a time. They will cover key verses and topics within each chapter that were life-changing then and are still life-changing today. They will inspire and encourage the "intentional" believer to move from a rut of complacency to a life that brings value to the Lord by how they live. This journey, will broaden and deepen our knowledge of God's expectations for each of us. We will learn the importance of obtaining the message from God's word and sustaining it daily through real-life application!

At the end of each chapter, as you pick up some missing nuggets in your life, you will have the opportunity to plant and share those nuggets that impacted you on our website—www.mondaybluestosundaypews.com. They will be stored like a journal and used as a testimony for others, and maybe as a reminder for you in the future. But most importantly, Monday Blues to Sunday Pews will donate over half of our proceeds to support the mission field, help the needy, and assist organizations in distributing God's word, globally. Remember this passage in Matt 16:24: *We're called to be intentional followers of Jesus Christ—daily!*

- Monday—Meditate on one Scripture in an area where you need help to refresh your mindset.

- Tuesday—Tell someone about your daily journey as you begin. Someone needs to hear it, too!

- Wednesday—Walk with a close friend and share your experience, as you're walking with God!

- Thursday—Thankful for one thing that happened this week. Showing gratitude is a huge step.

- Friday—Focus on another area in your life that needs improvement; we all have them.

- Saturday—Share one significant impact from the week with someone who also needs uplifting.

- Sunday—Serve in some capacity in your church or community—connect, serve, and grow.

God's Holiness
vs. Man's Lawlessness

A Guide through Leviticus

CARL BARRETT

Monday Blues to Sunday Pews

RESOURCE *Publications* · Eugene, Oregon

GOD'S HOLINESS VS. MAN'S LAWLESSNESS
A Guide through Leviticus

Monday Blues to Sunday Pews

Copyright © 2023 Carl Barrett. All rights reserved. Except for brief quotations in critical publications or reviews, no part of this book may be reproduced in any manner without prior written permission from the publisher. Write: Permissions, Wipf and Stock Publishers, 199 W. 8th Ave., Suite 3, Eugene, OR 97401.

Resource Publications
An Imprint of Wipf and Stock Publishers
199 W. 8th Ave., Suite 3
Eugene, OR 97401

www.wipfandstock.com

PAPERBACK ISBN: 978-1-6667-8466-4
HARDCOVER ISBN: 978-1-6667-8467-1
EBOOK ISBN: 978-1-6667-8468-8

08/22/23

Scripture quotations are taken from the Holy Bible, New Living Translation, copyright ©1996, 2004, 2015 by Tyndale House Foundation. Used by permission of Tyndale House Publishers, a Division of Tyndale House Ministries, Carol Stream, Illinois 60188. All rights reserved.

Contents

CONTENTS

Dedication

This book is dedicated to every Pastor, Evangelist, Missionary, Leader, Teacher, Personnel, and Volunteer positioned in the gap to defend God's Holiness. So, for the ones who are standing up for the Truth of God's word, abiding in Him, following and doing His work according to His command, at the disposal of His Spirit, and not wavering from His divine teachings and true nature, this is a massive shout-out for your selfless and ongoing pursuit of caring for the case and cause of Christ! In this world of escalating lawlessness, God needs willing, humble, fearless, bold, and confident servants to protect His most divine character, His holiness. In this darkened age, as His true children of the Light, it's imperative now more than ever that we are on the frontline of God's holiness, defending it with all the love, grace, and mercy He abounds. He's worthy of all our efforts toward the building of His Kingdom!

Romans 1:16–17, "For I am not ashamed of this Good News about Christ. It is the power of God at work, saving everyone who believes the Jew first and also the Gentile. This Good News tells us how God makes us right in his sight. This is accomplished from start to finish by faith. As the Scriptures say, "It is through faith that a righteous person has life."

Biography

Carl Barrett is the Founder and Executive Director of *Monday Blues to Sunday Pews Ministry*—partnering with other Christ-based organizations globally to help the needy, support the mission field, and increase the distribution of God's word worldwide. He's the author of *God Values Our Daily Steps, God's Guide to Freedom, God's People Count-Connecting God's Dots,* and *Searching for Your Comfort Zone.* In addition, he's the First Impressions Team Leader at Central Tyler Baptist Church in Tyler, Texas.

He has served as a Personal Development Mentor for the Texas Juvenile Justice Department and Prison Fellowship Ministries. He has been a chaplain, teacher, and preacher in multiple state penitentiaries and detention centers. He has also served as an instructor for National Fatherhood Initiative.

He holds a BSBA from Madison University. He studied biblical and theological studies at Texas Baptist Institute, An Introduction to C.S. Lewis at Hillsdale College, and Critical Issues in Christian Apologetics at Biola University. In addition, he has attended Dale Carnegie, Development Dimensions International, and Personal Dynamics Institute, where he studied human relations development, motivational leadership, and the empowerment of engagement.

Carl's aspiring passion is to help people apply the truth of God's word into their lives so they can live it out for the glory of God as representatives of Jesus Christ on this earth. He would tell you that it starts in our homes and then throughout our neighborhoods, community, church home, and abroad. *Our bio as Christlike followers is essential to our Lord and the building of His Kingdom in our everyday life!*

Commentaries

"We will always obey our Lord at all costs." That is the opposite of the spirit of lawlessness, which despises authority and cultivates chaos, division, and destruction. And there is no doubt that it is on the rise throughout this country and the world. In a time when unholiness is rampant in our homes, schools, communities, churches, and abroad, many Pastors and Leaders have alarming concerns about these escalating acts. They know that if we're not students of God's word, growing in His grace and love as believers, we can find ourselves vulnerable to the rise of lawlessness because it can distort our minds, heart, and attitude. So, it's vitally important that God's children are on the front line in pursuing God's most divine nature, with all the love, grace, and mercy He abounds. We must live the life He's prescribed since the beginning of time. See some comments from Pastors and Leaders from around the world below.

"We have a society today that is biblically illiterate. People do not understand God, His character, or His word; sadly, we see this in the church. Many Christians depend on a couple of hours a week in service or listening to anyone on social media. I pray and desire the church to know their Savior through His word. When we spend time in God's word, we learn His character and heart for His people. Knowing the Truth of His word will give you abundant, fruitful, and disciplined life in Jesus."

Pastor Kenny Pope
Calvary Plymouth England

"Man's spite for the holy law of God is an escalating problem of our time. The Ten Commandments have been removed from Court Houses, Schools, and the Public Square. Lawlessness has many causes. Lust of the eye, the lust of the flesh, and the pride of life are primary. Religiously supported Lawlessness is sustained with a false assumption that law justifies it." My father often stated, *"One cannot legislate righteous. "*Galatians 2:6.

"The conflation of salvation and holiness promotes bad doctrine and the loss of the true foundation of holiness, which is Jesus (He who saves). The law does not save. It reveals sinfulness. Therefore, there is tremendous pushback from our lost society and our religious communities. The Law shuts the mouth of the self-righteous, convincing them of sin." Romans 3

"Until then, the Redeemed must be called to quietness and contentment in the Potter's hand. He is the one who forms us into holiness. During formation, He uses us as a witness to the lawlessness of our time. We must bear the cross of selflessness in following Him who saves. Being quiet and content in His hand is the power, "strength" of the process of God forming us into His holy image." Isaiah 30:15

Paul Sudbrock, Church Planting Missionary, Baptist Bible Fellowship International
Studied Biblical Hebrew at The Hebrew University of Jerusalem
Studied Theology at the Baptist Bible Graduate School of Theology

"I believe the escalation of lawlessness in our country is directly related to Christians' lack of personal evangelism. The hypocrisy of many Christians has also led to a lack of influence on our culture."

Dr. Mark Forrest
Senior Pastor Lakeside Baptist Church, Granbury, Texas
Studied Theology at Southwestern Baptist Theological Seminary

One of the things clear in scripture is that sin brings pain, hurt, and brokenness. Part of God's intention in having us live in righteousness is so that we can enjoy the best of what He has created. He desires that we live in Shalom, wholeness, and peace in this world. Sin destroys and distorts the plan that God created for us. It always keeps us from enjoying the best things, the things that bring peace, significance, and security in this life, the things our heart truly craves. That is where the downward spiral starts, looking for these things in all the wrong places. When we look for these things in the unrighteous things of life that lead to more brokenness, lack of peace, lack of significance, and security, this emptiness causes us to look to even more unrighteous ways and things, trying to find what our heart desires. I think our culture today is the poster child for this downward spiral God warns us of in scripture.

In His grace, He continually and gently calls us back to following Him, knowing Him, to living a righteous life because He knows that is where we will find the things our soul craves. To know Him and walk in His way is where we can live this life with Shalom. Our hearts will be at peace with Him, as well as with others. We will find our meaning, purpose, significance, and security in the disciplines of righteousness, walking in His way and in relationship with Him.

Steve Engram
Senior Pastor – Desert Springs Community Church
Goodyear, Az.
Studied at Moody Bible Institute

In Isaiah 26:9, the Prophet stated, "At night my soul longs for Thee. Indeed, my spirit within me seeks Thee diligently; For when the earth experiences Your judgments, the inhabitants of the world learn righteousness." I find myself these days feeling the same way the Prophet Isaiah felt when he penned the words in this verse. As a Christian, it's hard to see the biblical values that have been the bedrock of our nation being thrown away like trash. It's even more difficult to see these biblical values being set aside by so many churches. When mainline denominations are debating biblical marriage and issues related to gender identity and evangelical pastors and church leaders are afraid to take issue with things that are immoral and ungodly because of the fear of being disliked, we are in trouble. I recently read, "If Paul were alive today in America, the church would receive a letter!"

Pastor Tommy Rush
First Baptist Church
Natchitoches, La

2 Pet 3:3–7, "Most importantly, I want to remind you that in the last days, scoffers will come, mocking the truth and following their own desires. They will say, "What happened to the promise that Jesus is coming again? From before the times of our ancestors, everything has remained the same since the world was first created." They deliberately forget that God made the heavens long ago by the word of his command, and he brought the earth out from the water and surrounded it with water. Then he used the water to destroy the ancient world with a mighty flood. And by the same word, the present heavens and earth have been stored up for fire. They are being kept for the day of judgment when ungodly people will be destroyed."

From these comments above, it is apparent that Christian Leaders worldwide are concerned about the escalation of evilness we're seeing today—and how it can affect the body of Christ. As God's children, we cannot afford to live in a bubble of complacency and comfort—because we're up against a world of complete defiance that opposes the very nature of God, our Lord Jesus Christ, the Spirit, and you and me. It's time for us to rise above the call.

An Ear for Holiness

In these days of unrighteous acts, our Heavenly Father is crying out to you and me, telling us to wake up, listen to His voice and take the necessary steps and measures—because His time of holiness is of the essence now. Throughout the scriptures, God draws attention to the discerning and attentive listener of His word for a reason. In Rev 2:7, He reminds us, *"Anyone with ears to hear must listen to the Spirit and understand what he is saying to the churches. To everyone who is victorious, I will give fruit from the tree of life in the paradise of God"*.

These times of spiritual disturbance today are challenging and require our immediate, undivided attention. So, we need to lend an ear to the power of God's word and the Holy Spirit with a pressing sense of urgency to respond earnestly. Now more than ever, we must heed His direction and guidance as His devoted children. Why? Because there is a divine essence of God needed in so many lives to survive spiritually in these days of lawlessness, and that's His "Holiness!"

Whenever our Lord Jesus says, "He who has ears to hear, let him hear," He's calling for His people to pay careful attention to a matter." It's another way of saying, "Listen up! Pay close attention!" He's speaking to those who have been given the word of God and possess every resource for living a godly life. But are we genuinely listening to the voice of our Lord in these final days? Jesus requests that we use our God-given senses (eyes to see, ears to hear, a discerning heart and mind) to tune in to His message and take notice of His commands with urgency.

God's word reminds us in Mk 4:21–23, "Then Jesus asked them, "Would anyone light a lamp and then put it under a basket or under a bed? Of course not! A lamp is placed on a stand, where its light will shine. For everything that is hidden will eventually be brought into the open, and every secret will be brought to light. Anyone with ears to hear should listen and understand."

In this powerful parable, Jesus is telling you and me that if we're not exposing His holy word to a world of corruption, we are fruitless and bringing no value to the Kingdom. We will discover in this book that if we're complacent Christians and "not" removing unholy things from our lives that may be preventing us from sharing the holiness of God with others, we are stepping into the caution zone of being lukewarm. And when that happens, we are useless to our Lord in a time where He needs us the most! If our love for the Lord is genuine, we will represent Him in these days of wickedness to its fullest. The Light of Christ needs to be exposed more than ever in these final days. Why?

Because in today's culture, we are seeing and experiencing clouds of darkness and evilness like never before. It seems to be taking over all the divine ways God designed since the beginning of His creation—because God's most precious nature has been abused and reused for acts of godlessness. People are taking God's holy name in vain to the magnitude of absolute corruptness by their actions. So, how are we, as His children, to respond during these days of unrighteousness?

By its very nature, light is meant to be revealed, and in a spiritual sense, we are His light in this dark world. As Christians, we must not hide the truth of this light stored and treasured within us. If you and I have the Truth of God and the power of His Spirit actively at work in our lives, we have an awe-inspiring responsibility to spread it in whatever way God gives us an opportunity.

Look at it this way. It is the same as someone who has a cure for a life-threatening disease. They have the moral responsibility to spread that cure to those needing healing immediately. God didn't light our spiritual lamps so that they would remain hidden from the world. If we see the demise of this world spiritually crumbling before our very eyes, it is time for us to use our ears and listen to God's message and put it to use. But the critical question is this: Are we genuinely listening to His voice?

A godly listener possesses a heart of humility and does not allow distractions to prevent them from heeding the voice of God. Their hearts and minds focus on the Lord's desires and not the disorderly conduct that's taking place in the world. No matter what, they're attentive to His guidance in everyday life. They embody patience and an intense pursuit and longing for His next steps. This is all because of one major component: their sincere love for His commands. Christians who are genuinely listening to the voice of God are in tune with His word and not grieving the Holy Spirit. They are putting forth an all-out effort to be prepared and ready to defend the faith at all costs.

Seeking God's truth takes time, energy, focus, and a willingness to be challenged and changed for a good reason. This is imperative for believers because He has a divine purpose and plan for you and me in today's culture. And if there was ever a time to pay attention to His word and occurrences around us, it is now! In less than six months of this new year, something is happening from the world of darkness to the spiritual realms—Good vs. evil is definitely on the battlefield.

People are parading wickedness all across TV and social media. And even here in our own country, our leaders allow treachery and evil to walk on the grounds of our nation's capital. We're constantly bombarded with man's intentional acts of irreverence and perverseness daily as if they are testing God's threshold. Their actions are trampling on the very foundation of God's word!

And just when you think it cannot get any worse, we hear of another new way of sinning. Rom 1:30–31 reminds us, "They are backstabbers, haters of God, insolent, proud, and boastful. They invent new ways of sinning, and they disobey their parents. They refuse to understand, break their promises, are heartless, and have no mercy." All of this corruption can lead us to depths of discouragement, disappointment, and even anger.

But God knows how to counter evilness with His own plans for good—because He assures us that He is still in control and has absolute power over all things. On the first Monday of 2023, millions of people (around the world) witnessed an NFL player die on a football field. When many thought this young man would not make it, God had a plan. We observed mainstream news brought to its very knees.

We witnessed people on a top-rated TV program stop dead in their tracks and pray on national TV for this player. When doctors and many experts thought the worst, God returned this young man to life, ready for action on the football field again. God is amazing and knows how to respond during our deepest despair. Undoubtedly, God is at work and causing or allowing things to happen for a reason! Who is paying attention? Unless we're asleep under a rock, we need to wake up. Because there is a spiritual battle taking place in our communities across the country and the world. Once again, God is calling out to those with open ears willing to listen and act!

Another event that got millions of people's attention in February 2023 was the massive earthquake and aftershock in the Turkey-Syria region. This tragic event was recorded as the worst natural casualty in over 100 years. One city affected by the Turkey earthquake holds biblical significance, Antioch. It played a prominent role in the life of the apostle Paul and served as a foundation for the early Church. According to the New Testament Book of Acts, in Antioch, followers of Jesus Christ were first called Christians.

Unfortunately, the recent earthquake has all but wiped out the city. But here's an amazing fact about Antioch. In the over twenty-four hundred years of destruction that has taken place in this area, God, in all His grace, has a way of restoring this most precious place of biblical history.

In the same way God allows evil people to commit wicked acts, He also allows the earth to reflect the consequences that sin has had on creation since the fall of man. Such events can rattle our spiritual cage, shake our confidence in this life, and force us to place our thoughts on the realities of Heaven and not this earth.

In Colossians chapter three, Paul provides a beautiful picture of fixing our thoughts on these truths. When we establish a heavenly mindset versus one of the world, we are placing the priorities of Heaven into daily practice. When this thought process is our primary concern, it leads us to concentrate more on the eternal versus the temporal. And this can lead us all to a life of rest and peace, but it also prepares us for God's plan.

Always remember this promise—God is good and can bring great things out of terrible tragedies and evil acts for His glory (Rom 8:28). But when God causes or allows things to happen, He's trying to get our attention for a reason and a cause. All these events are not a coincidence because God sees what is happening with His people and country today! I can only envision this in my mind. Christ is sitting at the right hand of the throne, next to His Father, with one tear after another, dropping to the floors of Heaven in anguish, as if He was back in the Garden of Gethsemane.

Make no mistake; God the Father, Christ the Son, and the Holy Spirit are not pleased with all the unholy practices saturating us today. They are calling believers to intercede in the gap and bridge God's holiness in people's lives! As devout Christians, we're needed more than ever because an intense battle of spiritual warfare is spreading—where evil is trying to take over.

Example: Deep State agencies have encouraged and empowered anti-Christian forces to target Christians. In doing so, kids' Bibles are confiscated in schools, Christian hats are banned, and kids are told they "Can't talk about Jesus." Churches are prohibited from using their property for worship and ministry, and a government agency even banned a realtor from saying, "Jesus loves you!" And to take it a step further, federal employees have been prohibited from attending Sunday church services. The church closures during the pandemic were just the beginning!

Unfortunately, we see a widespread escalation of similar targeted attacks on Christians and their core biblical beliefs everywhere.[1] I even read in an article that the Church of England is considering whether to stop referring to God as "He." This was a topic of significant discussion after priests asked to be allowed to use gender-neutral terms instead.

All around the world, there is an epidemic of depraved and reprobate minds that is unrestrained, unchecked, and out of control! We see God's most

---

1. American Center for Law and Justice, "Kids' Bibles Confiscated."

divine creation of humans being deformed and reformed to the ways of man's liking, not God's design. We're facing an ungodly wave that does not want to receive the love of the Truth, which means pursuing God's holiness is growing cold.

People have lost sight of godly values and have no regard for a fresh and newness of life in Jesus Christ! God's word told us beforehand in 1 Cor 1:18-31 that the worldly man has been blinded from the Truth and fallen into a foolish stupor—there are no attempts of true worship and praise. It's more about power, intellect, influence, and self.

In this passage above, Paul describes the spiritual condition of people unable or unwilling to perceive and even receive divine revelation and the absolute Truth! And that's why we see the elevating acts of lawlessness against Christians. God's children must stand up and stand out so the unbelieving world will know Whom we claim and represent!

But, regardless of the flying arrows coming our way, you and I are charged to progress and not regress like this nation. We are entrusted to be God's Citizens of Heaven and His children of Light in this dark world. We are His appointed ambassadors and representatives, not partly but wholly. We should be committed to His service each day of our lives. We must embrace and engage our real life in Jesus Christ more than ever. We need to breathe and live every day that He's endowed us on this earth while pressing forward in a manner He desires from you and me.

The genuine Christian possesses the nature of Jesus Christ living in them—because they hate the deeds of lawlessness and long to live a life pleasing to their Lord and Savior. They understand and know they will never reach perfection, but they continue to strive for God's standards, regardless (Phil 3:12–17)! Unfortunately, it seems more than ever that many Christians do not understand God's most divine nature of holiness. They are unwilling to lend an open ear, heart, and mind to the truth of God's word! Look at some of the profound evidence below.

A nationwide survey by The Barna Group on "The Concept of Holiness Baffles America" will be quite disturbing because it indicates that most adults need clarification, if not daunted, by the concept of holiness. But first, let me show you the biblical definition of the word holy or holiness, which is someone that is set apart (sanctified) and dedicated to serving and fulfilling the will of God. This means God considers them righteous, sacred, blameless, pure, and ready for His use! Pretty basic, straightforward, and elementary.

In the survey, one critical question posed to the polled people was: "What is the meaning of Holiness?" When pressed to describe what it means, adults gave a wide range of answers. The most common reply was "I don't know," offered by one out of every five adults (21%). Answers to this most critical question were across the board, and the most compelling results showed this disturbing fact; the born-again Christian's concept was the same as the non-born-again unbelievers!

This is alarming and sad because the essential characteristic of God is His holiness, and every true believer should know this! If we, as proclaimed followers of Jesus Christ, don't connect with the true nature of God, there will always be a disconnect in our spiritual walk.

Another disturbing key focus in this survey was to gauge those who are "Not Obsessed with Holiness." While the Christian Church may embrace it, many Americans do not adopt it as a focal point of their faith development. This is partly because barely one-third of Americans (35%) contend that "God expects you to become holy." A larger share of the born-again public believes God has called them to holiness (46%), but that portion remains a minority of the born-again population. Really, 46%! This is nowhere close to 100%, which should be the Christian's daily benchmark in pursuing God's most divine element.

The key takeaway from these studies is this: When combined with existing knowledge about the state of faith in America, the new survey findings caused the survey's director, George Barna, to suggest that churches must take this body of information seriously regarding holiness. "Realize that the results portray a body of Christians who attend church and read the Bible but do not understand the concept or significance of God's precious nature. They do not personally desire it and therefore do little if anything to pursue it."

People need to move away from the "cheap grace" of theology and replace their self-absorption with an extreme focus on all of God's ways. If we "don't" align our hearts with the holiness of God, there will be a weak developing structure of God's most divine nature in the body of Christ. There must be an emphasis on the importance of spiritual sanctification, which is the ultimate blueprint for pursuing God's holiness.[2]

With the growing age of sinfulness and confusion against the principles of God, we mustn't allow the growth of our Christlikeness to go stale. We must steadfastly convey and portray every truth of His word and live by it daily. Our Lord compels us to remain faithful through all life's circumstances—and be accountable Christians in the face of this darkened culture.

When Satan tempted Christ in the wilderness, Jesus made this profound statement to the enemy in Matt 4:4, "People do not live by bread alone, but by every word that comes from the mouth of God." If God's children would

2. Barna, "Concept of Holiness."

reflect the fullness and wholeness of the Gospel in their daily lives, the world would have a hard time blocking us from doing the will of God!

It doesn't matter what evil forces try to thwart God's plan; no one and nothing can. God will work all things together for the good of those who love Him and are called according to His purpose and plan, and nothing will ever separate us from the love of God (Rom 8:28–39). Our life-changing decision to align our will with God's ways and to always trust Him will be rewarded.

Our good works of holiness will result from a genuine relationship with the Good Shepherd and reflect in our conduct, which is the opposite of the unregenerate world. As Christ-followers of righteousness, we've been set apart for something special, which will be revealed soon—so don't despair.

Because while many humans attempt to degenerate this society and culture, God has a different plan. Through the power of His Spirit, He wants to regenerate anyone with ears willing to hear His authentic voice! Time may be running out, but today is the day of service for believers—and salvation for the unbeliever!

Our Almighty God is not surprised by all the evilness consuming His children in today's culture. And He is fully aware of this battle between the principalities of darkness and His Spirit. But here's one important note: God's grace, mercy, and love will allow people to choose between His ways or not! This is vital because no one knows the time and hour, but with each passing day, the end is getting closer than ever!

I believe that in these last days, God is showing us unbelievable measures of patience for anyone with ears "who is willing to hear His voice." 2 Pet 3:8–9, "But you must not forget this one thing, dear friends: A day is like a thousand years to the Lord, and a thousand years is like a day. The Lord isn't really being slow about his promise, as some people think. No, he is being patient for your sake. He does not want anyone to be destroyed but wants everyone to repent."

But unfortunately, His words will fall upon many deaf ears. That's why His faithful ones must be an influencer of God's holiness in every life we encounter. As wickedness continues to become a stronghold in society, Christians must lend an ear to God and discern, engage, and enforce acts of holiness! It's time for action—because time is running out! The evidence is right before us and growing increasingly with each passing day. For me, it's heartbreaking to see the very structure of God's divine nature being spiritually ripped to shreds.

Psalm 10: 1–11, "O Lord, why do you stand so far away? Why do you hide when I am in trouble? The wicked arrogantly hunt down the poor. Let them be caught in the evil they plan for others. For they brag about their evil desires; they praise the greedy and curse the Lord. The wicked are too proud to seek God. They seem to think that God is dead. Yet they succeed in everything they do. They do not see your punishment awaiting them. They sneer at all their enemies. They think, "Nothing bad will ever happen to us! We will be free of trouble forever!" Their mouths are full of cursing, lies, and threats. Trouble and evil are on the tips of their tongues. They lurk in ambush in the villages, waiting to murder innocent people. They are always searching for helpless victims. Like lions crouched in hiding, they wait to pounce on the helpless. Like hunters, they capture the helpless and drag them away in nets. Their helpless victims are crushed; they fall beneath the strength of the wicked. The wicked think, "God isn't watching us! He has closed his eyes and won't even see what we do!"

These types of people are, unfortunately, in for a rude awakening! But you and I have a job to do in spreading the holiness of God to as many people as possible who want to listen to His voice in these last days.

Preface

The United States of America was once a nation of laws—but it is rapidly becoming lawless and creating new ways to sin against a Holy God. What is the cause of this fast-pacing downward trend? An Oliver North blog entitled: "Lawlessness in America: The Progressive Culture of Death" said this: The deteriorating state of law and order has people asking, "What is happening to our country?" The answer is simple: *We are all reaping what "progressives" have sewn by 'devaluing human life.' A tragic consequence of the devaluation of human life is the culture of death now pervading American society. When our political leaders legalize the murder of innocent, unborn children, should anyone be surprised when murder becomes mundane?*[1]

When we, as a society and culture, devalue the human life God created, we have entirely taken God out of the equation. Because unfortunately, humans desire and want to choose a lifestyle based on their opinions, thoughts, attitudes, and way of living, not God's ways. When we reduce the worth of God's creation, it's an ejection of Him from every part of life. In other words, we have banished our Heavenly Father from the face of everything.

It's clear that the attacks against the complete design of our Almighty God are out to destroy the very fabric of His divine creation! We see these effects in our homes, schools, communities, states, and globally. And unfortunately, some churches are subtly removing the works of our Creator from the very structure He designed for personal fellowship and worship. Instead of honoring Him, we are defaming His name!

Why this escalation? Because it's biblically sound! As we approach the end of this age, we will be consumed with a Christ-hating, self-absorbed, self-deceived, and lawless world that is taking precedence over institutions and individuals so rapidly. An accurate diagnosis of the condition of humankind's actions can be best defined as heartless and inhumane—because people's disobedience against God is reaching epidemic proportions. What we're seeing

---

1. North and Goetsch, "Lawlessness in America."

in this end-time phase is the rapid increase of godless perversion that's out-pacing Christian conversion! (2 Tim 3:1)

Yes, it will be too often in this life when we'll feel the spiritual strains of persistent evil confronting our lives. Why? Because they continue to adopt and incorporate behaviors opposite our Christlike beliefs. But take rest in knowing that God's word confirmed these things would happen—and during these times, we should pray for His divine guidance with confidence.

Undoubtedly, we're up against an enraging tide that will only end after our upstream marathon is over. So, in this world of muted virtue, how can we, as God's holy people, overcome this powerful evil force that is increasing daily? Because sadly, we are witnessing a fallen world defying and denying a Holy God—by downgrading the very life He created at every beating turn. There is no doubt that we have some spiritual challenges ahead of us.

Since we are created in His image, our lives have deep-rooted and im-measurable value, but this culture overlooks this vital point. They ignore the fact that God's word abounds in that He created us and endowed us with an eternal soul to glorify Him, not demeaning His name! The Creator of you and I value our physical and spiritual life and gifted us to enjoy them. But in that enjoyment, we're to bring glory, honor, and praise to Him in how we live our lives. We must show actual value to our Heavenly Father by pursuing God's most compelling nature, His holiness!'

However, there's a different level of "personal pursuit" in our society. Be-cause it seems like every day, we hear leaders, politicians, and the mainstream media talk about the word "values." But really! What "values" could they pos-sibly be talking about? The truth is this. With the depravity and regression of human hearts, minds, and spirits, we don't have any "values" worth sharing with anyone—because today, godly standards are limited by humans' bad choices. The standard of living that our Creator ordained from the beginning of time has shifted to a way of life that has chosen to turn to the desires that please them most vs. a Holy God!

Scriptures tell us in 2 Timothy chapter 3 that people will be lovers of themselves, their money, and their possessions in the last days. They will be full of pride, unloving, unforgiven, slanderous, disobedient, ungrateful, un-teachable, cruel, arrogant, hate anything good, heretics, perverse, depraved, reckless, and love everything but God. They will act religious—but reject the very God that could make them godly. And this rejection has led to evil being manifested before us.

Now we face difficult times that are becoming more frequent with each passing day. More than ever, those weak in the flesh, unvirtuous, and lack-ing the knowledge of God's word will find themselves vulnerable to these dangerous tides of godlessness! So, we must keep spiritual sight and focus on the distinction between holiness and unholiness because it is apparent that many have lost the sense of God's most divine being. When we lose that sense spiritually and don't realize the difference between immoral and moral, we're in a danger zone! Why? Because people then cannot differentiate between right from wrong—or good from evil (Isa 5:20).

When we overlook the splendor of God, there will be an ugliness that creeps from the outside in—it will touch and affect our relationships in every way of life. That's why God commands us to reflect His nature, such as to be holy because He's holy, as He tells us in 1 Pet 1:15–16 and Lev 19:2. He shows us how to live this type of life fully and joyously through His Word and guidance by the Holy Spirit.

The author in Hebrews chapter 6:1-3 says, "So let us stop going over the basic teachings about Christ again and again. Let us go on instead and become mature in our understanding. Surely, we don't need to start again with the fundamental importance of repenting from evil deeds and placing our faith in God. You don't need further instruction about baptisms, the laying on of hands, the resurrection of the dead, and eternal judgment. And so, God willing, we will move forward to further understanding."

The bottom line is. There should be no excuse for God's genuine and faithful believers not striving for a life that is pleasing to Him (Rom 12:1). Why? Because a life of holiness is marked by gratitude to God! Peter reminds us in his second Epistle 1:3, "By his divine power, God has given us everything we need for living a godly life."

As Christ-followers, we pray for our country and its people to humble ourselves, turn away from our wicked deeds, and rediscover the godly values so needed in our lives, and that's under the authority of a Holy and Righteous God (2 Chr 16:9)! Because let's face it, there are short-term decisions that are having a long-term impact on people's lives. And over time, it is debilitating, deteriorating, and spiritually killing this society!

- From parents losing that natural affection for their own children.

- To the escalation of narcissism—an excessive self-interest.

- To the constant increase in teenagers' cruelty, bullying, and lack of respect.

- To our government making it legal for doctors and scientists to create "three-parent babies" in the United States.

- Crime across multiple categories is increasing.

- To the sexual perversion of all types skyrocketing off the charts.

- Men want to become women, women want to become men, and they want to ingrain this destruction in the lives of young children.

- To people who want to redefine marriage (versus how our Holy God intended).

- The surge of relationships between three people is so popular that dating websites have launched new ones to accommodate their desires.

- The rise of occults in this nation.

- Straying away from preaching and teaching the Truth of God's word.

- The United States claims the highest divorce rate in the world.

- Surging death rates from suicide, drug overdoses, and alcoholism, re-searchers refer to as "deaths of despair." The U.S. has one of the highest suicide rates among the wealthiest nations in the world.

- Over one hundred million people are affected by spousal, drug, sex, or alcohol abuse.

- And over 65 million babies have been aborted since 1973, 1 every 30 seconds!

God, help us and give us strength to inject a nation of evil with the life-saving image of Your holiness! Help us make the 'least of these' a priority in life today.

With this decline of godliness permeating so extensively, there should be an urging pursuit in every Christian to live out the fullness of God's most essential quality every day. Our consciousness should be riddled to the core of our soul and spirit, where we're moved with such a conviction that it will lead us to say, as Isaiah did, "Lord, I will go! Send me; I will be your messenger in these last days." No matter where the Lord is calling us today as His servants if there are no spiritual steps to God's holiness in our daily life, we will lose the spiritual, visible site of the life God desires.

This book will focus on the one primary attribute needed in every be-liever's life: Holiness. Why? Because it is fading away from the face of God's creation. We'll see the importance of putting on this armor and living it daily. Our faith in God should guide us in how we think and act in ways that are pleasing to Him—because today, there is very little that God would deem acceptable.

If we're not in line with God's core values, we will lose all moral views of our Creator and become muddied and distorted in our thought processes! He longs for us to channel acts of godliness throughout our homes and com-munity. We're not talking about perfection but a life that echoes genuine

Christlikeness. It starts with you and me taking ownership and being account-able for all our acts of holiness.

At the end of this journey, we will see the powerful impact of choice—because we're either living in the Spirit—or the flesh (Galatians chapter 5). Are you pointed toward His Righteousness in this constant battle of spiritual sur-vival? Because as our time as His dedicated servants on this earth comes closer to an end, our spiritual choices will show where our true loyalty lies: Either under the authority of a Holy God—or the unholiness and lawlessness of this dying world. Our spiritual survival hinges on critical choices of God's holiness each day of our life. It must be taken seriously and to extreme measures in this world of darkness, and it starts with you and me!

Introduction

"Survival of the Fittest" is an adage coined by the English sociologist and philosopher Herbert Spencer in his 1864 book, *"Principles of Biology,"* after reading the work of evolutionist Charles Darwin. But if we think about it, *Survivor of the Fittest* started after man's fall in the Garden of Eden. We were perfectly fit when God created man and woman. But Adam and Eve allowed the enemy to sway them from God's perfect design to a corruptible and imperfect state. And this led to our unfit status in the eyes of our Heavenly Creator.

And since that turn of events, it is now the *"Survival of the spiritually weak!"* Jesus reminds us, *"My strength is made perfect in your weakness,* (2 Cor 12:9). Think about the power of those words. The same Spirit that raised Christ from the dead indwells in you and me as believers in Jesus Christ.

We have no strength (on our own) to survive in a world that has fallen from the standards of God's ways. Only Jesus has been able to do this for us. In all His weakness on that cross, He succeeded the will of His Father for you and me. He then became our *Survivor of the Perfect Fit.* And when we're humble and living for Him, we finally realize it is no longer about us, but Christ living in you and me (Gal 2:20). Because He is our perfect fit for a holy life!

My last books, "God Values Our Daily Steps" and "God's Guide to Freedom," focused on the importance of applying God's word in our daily life. We looked at ways where God can help us overcome areas of weakness and live out a life of liberty that God intended, portraying all His divine nature— *Christlikeness in its purest form!* And the dovetail from those books to this one is layered on the foundation of *God's holiness.*

Why is this essential attribute so important? In a real sense, *holiness is the foundation of God's life, His true character.* It's that nature which gives complete unity to His divine being. It comprises His righteousness, graciousness, goodness, and lovingkindness—*but hatred of evil.* God's word reminds us in *Hab* 1:13, *"But you are pure and cannot stand the sight of evil. Will you wink at their treachery? Should you be silent while the wicked swallow up people more righteous than they?"*

God's very qualities are made of holiness, as light is the essence of the sun. And for that reason, we think of His most divine nature not so much as an attribute of God, like wisdom, love, or mercy, *but as the summation of all His features. It's the outshining and pouring out of all that God is!*

And this is important for us to understand as believers—because here's the gut-punch question. How does this world sum you and me up as followers and leaders of Jesus Christ? *Do they see the fullness of God shining and pouring out His true nature in our daily life? Do they see the Fruit of the Spirit actively at work in and through us?*

We must be determined and dedicated with all our heart, soul, mind, and strength in this ongoing challenge and pursuit of holiness by:

- Yielding to the power of the Holy Spirit; Rom 8:16, Gal 5:22, 23, Heb 12:11

- Filling our minds with the Word of God; Psalm 1, Heb 8:10, Col 3:16

- Having a repentant heart; 2 Cor 7:9-11, Joel 2:12-13, Ps 51:17, 2 Tim 2:25

- Abstaining from all evil; 1 Thess 4:3-8, 1 Thess 5:22-24, 1 Pet 1:14–16, Eph 5:11

- Dying to self; Matt 16:24-25, 2 Cor 5:17, Gal 2:20, Gal 5:24, 1 Cor 2:14

- Incorporating a fervent prayer life; 1 Tim 2:1-6, Phil 4:6, Ps 145:18, 1 John 5:14

- Guarding our hearts; Phil 4:6-7, Prov 4:23, Ps 51:10, Ps 73:26

- Being conscious of our attitude; Phil 2:5, 2:14, Eph 4:23, 1 Pet 4:1, Rom 15:5

- Holding ourselves as accountable Christians; Gal 5:25-26, Rom 14:12

- Possessing a heart full of thanksgiving and praise; Ps 7:17, Col 3:15, 1 Thess 5:18

- Being content; 1 Tim 6:6, Heb 13:5, Matt 6:33, Phil 4:11, 2 Cor 12:10, Eccl 3:12-13

- Pursuing God's Holiness at all costs; Heb 12:14, 2 Cor 7:1, Rom 6:22, 2 Tim 2:21, 1 Pet 2:9, 1 Thess 4:7

We must instill an absolute resolve to attain our goals of godliness in life at all costs. No matter the obstacles in this world that will confront us, we must move forward through all the barriers, *fearlessly and graciously, by the power of God.*

God's Holiness vs. Man's Lawlessness will uncover the realities of sinful acts saturating our lives *that the Bible describes as our last days.* However, the game-changer for believers will be this: "Is the outward appearance of people who call themselves *Christians aligned with the actual inner working of His Spirit?"*

Because if we're not allowing the power of God's Spirit to lead us, and we ignore the truth of His word, what will ensue is chaos, confusion, and division. This is the outcome when God's holiness is absent in people's hearts, minds, and spirits. But in God's boundless grace, mercy, and love, His word connects man's rebellious ways with his need for God's forgiveness.

But when our sinful desires counter the ways of God, it's an open invitation to evil because it removes anything godly in His prescriptive plan for holiness. This open door of corruption occurs when we deprive God's righteous and pure ways of living—and it can lead anyone to spiritual impoverishment, affliction, and distress. It's a complete "lack" of seeking God's blessings in our lives, which is needed in the hearts of His children. Ephesians 1:3 says that we have been blessed with all spiritual blessings in Christ as our Lord, which is the key to our relationship with God through Jesus Christ. These benefits include being chosen, adopted, accepted, redeemed, forgiven for our sins, sealed by the Spirit, and given His wisdom and insight through the power of His word!

And this all comes to us because of God's "grace," which means "favor, blessing, or kindness." We can all extend grace to others, but when the word *grace* is used in connection with God, it takes on a more powerful meaning. Grace is God choosing to bless us rather than curse us as our sin deserves; it is His lovingkindness to the undeserving. We have an unbounded privilege in our Savior and King when we choose to follow Him; they are countless. These are all available through that right relationship with Jesus Christ, which involves repenting and turning away from all lawless deeds that can separate us from God. Who would not aspire to these unimaginable blessings from a Loving and Wonderful Creator?

But unfortunately, even with all of God's grace, our fight against the ways of man's lawless currents continues! And this battle of spiritual warfare that we, as Christians, are going through reminds me of this article about the life of a salmon. This is fascinating because it strikingly portrays some interesting parallels in our struggle as Christians today.

Sometimes the salmon go through their normal life cycle as eggs and fingerlings from the freshwater rivers and eventually live in the sea. But once they reach maturity, they have an absolute resolve to return to their spawning grounds, hundreds or thousands of kilometers away. Unfortunately, the trip back to their spawning grounds is seemingly impossible, full of dangers, traps, and obstacles, as they will swim against the rivers' overbearing currents.

Many of the salmon die returning to their grounds; bears and birds of prey catch them and eat them. Some of them hit rocks, logs, and other obstacles. Sometimes they must swim through shallow waters to get through their journey. But they never stop or rest from swimming against the current. Otherwise, it would carry them away from their destination. The incredible thing is, for them to reach their spawning grounds, they must jump upstream, up against a waterfall, and sometimes more than once in their journey. Many of their jumps fail, but they persist until they get through the waterfall or die trying.

Against all odds, many eventually reach their spawning grounds, and a new generation of salmon eggs are laid and later hatch to become fingerlings. Without their unbelievable and undeniable endurance and perseverance, many salmon and future generations would never have experienced life in the waters. We can count ourselves lucky not to be a salmon! But as Christians, compared to salmon, we have a higher calling, and we're held to a higher standard despite the various fronts we will face in life's journey.[1]

Just like the life of the salmon, our flesh is up against all odds because it is prone to want what it wants. In Rom 7:21–25, Paul admits his constant battle between flesh and spirit. "I have discovered this principle of life—that when I want to do what is right, I inevitably do what is wrong. I love God's law with all my heart. But there is another power within me that is at war with my mind. This power makes me a slave to the sin that is still within me. Oh, what a miserable person I am! Who will free me from this life that is dominated by sin and death? Thank God! The answer is in Jesus Christ, our Lord. So, you see how it is: In my mind, I really want to obey God's law, but because of my sinful nature, I am a slave to sin."

Each battle with temptation is won or lost based on how fully we are surrendered to the control of the Holy Spirit (Gal 5:16–26). In Rom 6:1–2, Paul asked, *"Well then, should we keep on sinning so that God can show us more and more of his wonderful grace? Of course not! Since we have died to sin, how can we continue to live in it?"* Although Christians will still sin after being saved, the heart change that the Spirit brings will result in a new attitude toward any acts of unholiness. How? Because lifestyles that oppose a Holy God cannot continue if we choose a Christian life. So, here's the gut punch: "If we've

---

1. Caballes, "Pursuing Holiness."

genuinely surrendered our whole lives to the Lord," we have a new boss in our life: His name is Jesus Christ![2] (Rom 10:9; Col 2:6)

The salmon reaching their spawning grounds are not optional; it's a matter of survival in their life's cycle, just like holiness is not an option for Christians in this life's journey. God issues a command through Peter that all Christians be holy because it characterizes everything we do as His chosen ones. God began teaching His people the meaning of holiness when He revealed Himself to Moses in the burning bush (Exod 3:1–6). God told Moses, "Do not come any closer," the Lord warned. "Take off your sandals, for you are standing on holy ground" (Exod 3:5).

Once again, why is God's most divine nature essential in our Christian lives? 1) It keeps us connected to God. 2) It sets us apart as righteous ones prepared to serve the Lord. 3) It shows that God possesses us, not the world. 4) It shows us the importance of obedience. 5) It exposes our sinful ways so we can come clean with God. And coming spiritually clean with God is vital because it's a step towards godliness and establishes a life of spiritual healthiness. It cleans out our dirty souls, spirit and mouths, and every inkling of filthiness in our lives.

When David asked God in Ps 51:10 to "Create in me a clean heart, O God. Renew a loyal spirit within me." He was convicted and led to see the impurity of his heart and nature, from which all his evil actions flowed. He knew that he could not make his heart clean; it was the work of God. But what I love about this passage is the second phase of it, "renew a loyal spirit within me."

Obviously, David was tired of his sinful nature and wanted to be cleansed by God. He was tired of his ill-spirited ways and desired to be restored, refreshed, and renewed. And just as important, David did not want to be a backslider because that is someone who reverts to bad habits and gives in to their temptations.

A backslider falls off the Christlike trail of holiness. And in time, they will possess a degenerate heart and spirit that will lead them astray from God's straight and narrow. And when that type of lifestyle of unrighteousness becomes habitual, they will lose that desire to come clean with God. We must understand this PowerPoint; God will not allow habitual sin in a Christian's life. 1 Cor 6:9–11, and Gal 5:19–21.

But God in all His Omnipotence, Omniscience, and Omnipresence foreknew this would happen with humans—because He tells us in Matt 7:13 *that the road to destruction is wide, while the path to Heaven is narrow. Jesus reminds us in Luke 12:49–56 that He did not come to bring peace but to divide people against each other. This is profound and should substantiate what God's*

2. Got Questions, "Do Christians Sin?"

word tells us: there will be two groups, one going one way and the other completely opposite.

Is it possible that we don't think about the great divide before us? This great divide finds on one side the redeemed of the Lord, those who follow all His righteous and holy ways of living, while on the other side are the hellbound, the ones who follow lawlessness and reject God's free gift of salvation through Jesus Christ. *Time is running out for the world, so the evidence of godliness should be depicted in His faithful children who claim they are on the "right side of God's great divide."*

But here's excellent news for anyone who wants to escape from their acts of lawless deeds! Once again, God's word reminds us in 2 Pet 3:8–15, He is not being slow about His promise, but He's being patient for our sake! If you find yourself on the wrong side of the great divide, He always has an open invitation for anyone ready and willing to take that leap of faith! And in the meantime, for His believers, He wants to find us living a peaceful life that is blameless, pure, ready, and prepared for His use.

If we know that we're God's chosen ones, as Paul states in Ephesians chapter one and Peter reminds us in 1 Pet 2:9, we must ensure that God's ways are displayed in our lives in these final days because it could be a life-changer for someone! God's word reminds us in Luke 15:7. *"In the same way, there is more joy in heaven over one lost sinner who repents and returns to God than over ninety-nine others who are righteous and haven't strayed away!"* Our simple acts of godliness each day could bring that one person into a new relationship with our Lord and Savior, Jesus Christ. *And today, that's as important as ever!*

If you feel far away from the holiness of an Almighty God, this daily guide through Leviticus can be your map of atonement (reparation for wrong). Because, just like the Israelites, God has redeemed and consecrated Christians for a reason. Jesus Christ offered Himself as the perfect sacrifice on our behalf, taking the punishment that we deserved so that we might be forgiven. Those who trust and believe by faith in Jesus' atoning act become God's children and are saved by God's grace (Eph 2:8–9).

And if we are indeed His children, He wants us to reflect His most essential nature in our everyday Christian walk. He is sanctifying you and me (setting us apart) like He did the nation of Israel for a purpose and plan that will glorify Him. So, we need to ask ourselves this question constantly. Does my life mirror His Son, Jesus Christ, daily? In what ways are we growing more like Christ?

Remember, we are not trying to live a holy life to earn salvation. Living a pure and blameless life is a natural outgrowth of being saved by God's grace, obeying His word, filled with His Spirit, and sanctified daily. And the outcome is a Christian who loves the Lord with all their heart, soul, mind, and strength.

It is also essential to not give up when we mess things up. Instead, when we fail, our response should be to confess the sin and keep moving forward in our Christian walk (1 John 1:9). Rom 8:1 says, *"There is now no condemnation for those who are in Christ Jesus."*[3] God's grace doesn't go away when we make mistakes, which should give us an undeniable motivation to take those necessary steps in our pursuit of God's holiness more than ever. Why? Because He's worthy of our efforts!

Isa 61:1–3, "The Spirit of the Sovereign LORD is upon me, for the LORD has anointed me to bring good news to the poor. He has sent me to comfort the brokenhearted and to proclaim that captives will be released and prisoners will be freed. He has sent me to tell those who mourn that the time of the LORD's favor has come and, with it, the day of God's anger against their enemies. To all who mourn in Israel, he will give a crown of beauty for ashes, a joyous blessing instead of mourning, festive praise instead of despair. In their righteousness, they will be like great oaks that the LORD has planted for his own glory."

3. Got Questions, "How Do I Live?"

Leviticus: The Book of Holiness

What a perfect book and guide that can show us the journey and path we need to be on in our daily life. Why? Because the overall message of Leviticus is the holiness of God, our sanctification stages, and how a sinful man can approach and *draw closer to an Almighty and Holy God.*

You can break Leviticus into two fractions: 1) obtaining the way to God (access) and then 2) walking with God through the process of sanctification. This book is God's guide for His newly redeemed people because it shows the Israelites: • *How to worship God.* • *How to serve God.* • *How to obey God, which are all critical areas that we need to incorporate into our daily lives.* This Old Testament book conveys the importance of this significant point; *once we receive God's forgiveness and acceptance, it should be followed by holy living and spiritual growth.*

The book of Leviticus was the first book studied by a Jewish child, yet it is often among the last books of the Bible to be studied by a Christian. It is probably the least popular and least-read book in the Bible. But that should not be the case because this essential book *mentions the word Holy more than any other book in the Bible.* "Holy" and "holiness" occur over 900 times in Scripture, and both the *Old and New Testaments speak more about holiness than any other attribute.* And holiness is in Leviticus 87 times. So, we can see why God's nature of holiness is critical and a key focus in this book.

Leviticus expands on the instructions for how God's people (Israel) *were to worship Him and Him alone and govern themselves under God's guidelines!* It lays forth the requirements of the sacrificial system that would allow God to overlook the sins of His people until the perfect and ultimate sacrifice of Jesus Christ would provide redemption and complete atonement for the sins of all of God's elect. God established the sacrificial system so His covenant people might enjoy His fellowship through worship, allowing repentance and renewal in their lives!

And this leads to another profound point in this excellent book: the process of sanctification. This is the growing phase of our Christian life that we desperately need. It is the spiritual exercise of becoming more like Christ by purifying our hearts and minds through repentance, prayer, and biblical application. Sanctification is vital to our life because it aligns us with God's will. Once we're saved by faith in Jesus Christ, we have the indwelling Spirit within us. We've been made new and transformed and now can achieve our spiritual goals through His strength. We start the journey of our Christian walk in the presence of a Holy God, where the world sees our spiritual growth.

Sanctification is the lifelong process by which we become holy. It becomes our ultimate purpose in everyday life because that's God's goal for you and me. Think of holiness in this way. *It's God's only intended destiny for you and me as followers of Christ. That's a power punch!* It comes by faith, love, and walking after the Spirit, and it's by faith a person receives the Holy Spirit, *which makes holiness possible.* Genuine saving faith in God will *inevitably include obedience to God and loving all His ways*!

We must remember this point: He came to save and redeem you and me *because He created us to be holy so we can display His one true and divine nature.* Once again, God's word reminds us powerfully in Lev 20:26: "*You must be holy because I, the Lord, am holy. I have set you apart from others to be my very own.*" "Holy" means "set apart," but it's much more involved than just being special. *God is holy: far greater in love, goodness, power, and justice than humans.*

God has made Israel His people and wants to set them apart from the pagan nations because His people now represent Him on earth. He has now established His presence in the Tabernacle, a portable holy place where God can dwell in the midst of His new nation. But if people live in God's presence, some things must change because God is so "other" from the world.

So, the people associated with Him also must become "others," too. **God is holy, and his people must also be holy, which requires living a life of spiritual cleanliness versus an unclean and immoral lifestyle![1]** Now that God had redeemed Israel, they would be *purified into a people worthy of their God.* In Leviticus, we learn that God loves to be approached, but on His terms—and this same approach applies to you and me!

In this compelling Old Testament book, we will see how Yahweh opened the way for the Israelites to come in the presence of a Holy God. Why did God do this? Because He desired His children to worship Him with their lives, sacrificially and selflessly. He provided detailed instructions for His children so they would know God's requirements for living responsible and accountable

1. Krantz, "Leviticus: How to Coexist."

lives in a pattern that applies to us today (Rom 12:1–2). We will see profound examples of a vertical relationship with our Lord that can have a horizontal impact on others around us. In this process, we glorify our Heavenly Father when our lives are aligned with Him.

Part of God's guidelines for His people during the Old Testament days were approximately 613 laws. *First,* they were established to reveal the divine character of God as a means for His people to unite with Him. Second, it would reveal the sinfulness of man and hold them accountable. Third, it would show them how to provide forgiveness through the sacrifice offerings and provide a way of worship through faith in His yearly events. Fourth, they would identify His children as His own and set them apart from other nations. Finally, it would illustrate physical and spiritual health directions and reveal that *no one can keep all His laws. Why? Because we all fall short of God's standards, and that is why* we need Him and all His holiness and righteousness in our daily life!

Another critical point of emphasis in this book is one of celebration. Leviticus provides us with instructions for the feasts. These were special occasions set aside for remembering what God had done for His children. It was a time of giving thanks and praise to Him while rededicating their lives to His service. As fellow believers in Christ today, we all deem special occasions as precious times to get together with our families. Still, we must incorporate more memorable days of worship, remembrance, fellowship, and celebration with all our brothers and sisters in Christ to keep God's goodness and loving-kindness fresh and alive daily!

When God set His chosen ones apart for His works of holiness, it communicates to us today that receiving God's forgiveness and acceptance "should be followed by sanctification." This is so important—because, as God's children, the working of His Spirit in our lives is living proof that we're maturing and spiritually growing in Christlikeness. Without this manifestation, there is no evidence of God at work in our lives.

Why is the sanctifying process so necessary? Because it aligns and links us to our Lord for His service and plan in our lives. This connection is our vital lifeline to have a fighting chance against the battles of unholiness. We will never have a chance on this side of heaven if the information we put into our ears, minds, hearts, and spirit is not biblically correct, pure, and holy. That is why our conscience (moral sense) and, most importantly, our consciousness (aware and alert) must be positioned with the power of God's word and His Spirit.

For us today, the purpose of the law was to point us to Christ. God gave the Law to define sin and demonstrate our need for an eternal Savior. And through His Spirit, His presence is available for anyone willing and ready to accept Him as their Lord. The number of 613 laws is insignificant (hallelujah), but *the number one (Jesus Christ) is significant!* How we abide in Him and Him in us by His word (John 15:4–11) is essential—because it depicts how we allow Him to govern our lives as Lord. And the beauty of this is when Christlikeness surfaces and comes alive in us, and the transparency of Jesus Christ is visible in our daily lives.

When we're walking in the holiness of God—we are walking in His love. This daily walk will elevate our faith and obedience—and lead us to joyful dependence on Him alone. This will help us to grasp more of God's wisdom and knowledge—and possess a discerning spirit that will enable us to avoid those grave dangers in everyday life.

When we allow the power of His word and Spirit to lead us each step of our daily lives—we will be more adept at defocusing from the toxic things in life and refocusing on the safety and security of God's blessings—that He has so richly conveyed in the Bible. What a journey this will be as we walk in the presence of our Holy God!

CHAPTER 1

Total Sacrifice

Lev 1:1-3, "The LORD called to Moses from the Tabernacle and said to him, "Give the following instructions to the people of Israel. When you present an animal as an offering to the LORD, you may take it from your herd of cattle or your flock of sheep and goats. "If the animal you present as a burnt offering is from the herd, it must be a male with no defects. Bring it to the entrance of the Tabernacle so the Lord may accept you."

God is profoundly setting the precedence in this first chapter. For it was no sooner did the cloud of Glory come down and rested on the Tabernacle—that Yahweh would tell Moses how it was to be used in genuine worship with Him. As we will see in this powerful book (one chapter at a time), no one can approach a Holy God and be in His presence when there is sin; it must be dealt with!

Animals for the Burnt Offering were always male and domesticated; they were not wild or untamed. The blood of the animal sacrifices covered that person's sin, allowing them to draw near to the Holy God of Israel. However, that person could only be forgiven for their sins through complete repentance and by returning to the ways of God! The sacrifice or offering was the only way a person could approach God and restore their relationship with Him.

A "whole" burnt offering described later in Chapter One was a voluntary act of worship expressing devotion or commitment to God. Each of these sacrifices involved certain elements and had a specific purpose—whether animals or fruit of the field. Most were split into two or three portions; God's part, the portion for the Levites or priests, and if there was a third, a piece kept by the person offering the sacrifice. God provided very detailed instructions for each

1

offering because He was teaching His children a brand-new way of life, which would cleanse them of many pagan practices that were ingrained in their lives. After all, He wanted them to be set apart from the pagans as His own.

Every detail God provided to the Israelites on His requirements for each offering would prevent them from slipping back into those corrupt ways of living—"if they obeyed His commands." Reading some of the graphic portrayals of these sacrifices paints a central theme of the seriousness of sin and God's incredible mercy! Bottom line. God had to start from scratch with the Israelites—as He does with many of us today.

The burnt offering is one of history's oldest and most common offerings. It was intended as an atoning and total sacrifice because the individual recognized and acknowledged that their action should have resulted in death. This is why they touched the head of the animal—it was a necessary and symbolic transfer of their sins to the innocent creature.

The main reason God commanded an animal with no defects is that it had to be clean and pure to transfer the guilt and shame of the sinner to the purity and innocence of that living animal. An imperfect sacrifice could not satisfy the atonement of any sin. A person could give a burnt offering any time—because a sacrifice of general atonement was basically unlimited! It was an admission of their sinful nature and a request for a renewed relationship with God.

As a believer in Jesus Christ today, do you ever feel like you're in a spiritual rut and need a renewed relationship with your Lord? Is the act of that same sin getting old, beating you down, and creating a distance between you and Christ? Do you feel like (at times) your Christian life is not progressing? While the sacrifice was significant in the Old Testament, God clarified that the critical component in coming clean and moving forward with Him lies in the obedience of our hearts. "Obedience from the heart means we're bondservants of the Lord, no one or nothing else; we're committed to doing the will of God from the heart." Eph 6:5–6.

To attain the level of a bondservant of Jesus Christ, we must be transformed, living in a manner that honors Him, which only comes when we submit our "whole" selves to the working of His Spirit. Simply put, moving from a theological point to a practical purpose of application in our lives as God's children. God's word reminds us in Hebrews chapter six that we should not find ourselves going back over the basics of Christianity but let us go on and become mature in our understanding. Surely, we don't need to start all over again with the importance of turning away from our evil deeds!

Romans 12: 1–2 gives us powerful insight into how we're to offer our bodies as total sacrifices to God, living in a way that glorifies Him, the kind

He will accept. A large nugget in this passage, which shows us an area that can lead us "from not living a holy life," is this; when we allow the world and flesh to consume our minds and distort our path.

So, you ask, what is the key to moving from this old way of life? And that key component is discernment (set apart). What do I mean? We must train our conscience, heart, mind, and body to distinguish right from wrong. We must grasp and comprehend the things obscuring in this crazed culture that we live in today. This is the quality of godliness we all need—because the ways of this world are spiritually confusing and complicated. Spiritual discernment is a treasured gift because it is the ability to tell the difference between truth and error. And most importantly, it is essential in our Christian life so we can possess the wisdom of God.

The only way to grow in this area of our lives is first to recognize that God is the only One who can increase wisdom, and that's why we must pray for it (Jas 1:5; Phil 1:9). Then, as we start to know and grow in the wisdom of God, we can distinguish good from evil. This does not happen overnight; it is part of our sanctification stages in our walk with the Lord. Through this training and practice exercise, we pay attention to the Scripture, go to the Bible as our primary source, learn the truth, and, by meditation on the Word, we apply and reinforce it in our lives (2 Pet 1:3–21).

To develop this essential quality in our Christian life is to know the absolute authenticity of the truth so that when the false appears, we can recognize it. Understanding the true meaning of God's word, obeying it, and leaning to the Holy Spirit for guidance will help us be more trained by constant practice so we can distinguish good vs. evil.

During this process, we will know God's character and will for our lives. The heart of spiritual discernment is distinguishing the voice of the world from the voice of God to have a sense that this is right or "this is wrong." It fends off temptation and allows us to "hate what is evil; and cling to what is good" (Rom 12:9).[1]

As believers, we have access to God's resources that help us to live the life He desires (2 Peter chapter one). Throughout the Old Testament, we see times when there was a distance between God and His children. And that distance was because of their sinful ways and not coming clean with an all-out attempt to draw near to God.

And unfortunately, many today feel far away from their Heavenly Father, as if He's silent or absent. The excellent parallel for us, just like in the book of Leviticus, is if we're not walking in obedience and holiness, there is a barrier

---

1. Got Questions, "Spiritual Discernment."

that will separate us from Him called sin! If we want more of His presence in our life, we must come out of the darkness that's blinding us.

When we're going through sanctification, and our hearts are in tune with Him, He will shed more of His light for us to see things more clearly. However, if we allow the cares of this world to distort our minds and thought processes, which make us ill-spirited, we plug up our spiritual ears, and we will not hear God through His word. That is so prevalent in Christians today; they're more in tune with the news, social media, and all the theories of man, but not the truth of God's word. As Christians, we must know this fundamental fact—His Spirit speaks to us through God's Holy word. And in that word, we have the truth and "Words of Life."

A devoted person to the Lord is fully committed to His ways, where He gets most of their time and attention. When we allow our Lord through the power of His Spirit to shape us and mold us to be more Christlike, our mind-set of genuine commitment becomes second nature, like walking with Him throughout the day (just like breathing air). The more quality time we spend with our Lord, the less time we'll have to dabble in ways that are not pleasing to Him.

Eph 5:5–10, "You can be sure that no immoral, impure, or greedy person will inherit the Kingdom of Christ and of God. For a greedy person is an idolater, worshiping the things of this world. Don't be fooled by those who try to excuse these sins, for the anger of God will fall on all who disobey him. Don't participate in the things these people do. For once, you were full of darkness, but now you have light from the Lord. So, live as people of light! For this light within you produces only what is good and right and true. Carefully determine what pleases the Lord. Take no part in the worthless deeds of evil and darkness; instead, expose them."

CHAPTER 2

Our Best

Lev 2:1–2, "When you present grain as an offering to the LORD, the offering must consist of choice flour. You are to pour olive oil on it, sprinkle it with frankincense, and bring it to Aaron's sons, the priests. The priest will scoop out a handful of the flour moistened with oil, "together" with all the frankincense, and burn this 'representative portion' on the altar. It is a 'special gift,' a pleasing aroma to the LORD."

Just like the whole burnt offering, the grain offering was also voluntary, in which the fruit of the field was offered as a cake or baked bread made of grain with the finest flour, oil, and salt. Fine flour is perfect in its quality of evenness, tenderness, and gentleness because the grain is finely crushed and sifted, which would yield a superior standard! This offering was their gift of thanksgiving to God—because it was a simple reminder that their food and all they possessed came from Yahweh. It was their genuine acknowledgment and means of showing honor and respect to their Almighty God.

The grain offering is described as the holiest part of the food offerings presented to the Lord (Lev 2:10)—because it comprises choice flour, olive oil poured on it, and is sprinkled with frankincense. The olive oil physically represents the priest's responsibility, glory, and authority, while the frankincense symbolizes holy and righteousness. This combined formula brought forth a pleasing and sweet aroma to God. And here's a keynote. The grain offering could be personalized in its presentation because it was to be given out of a person's free will.

But, just as true worship is our free will offering to the Lord, it pleases our Heavenly Father when it's from an obedient and contrite heart. And this

5

personal formula is required in our daily life, which should consist of our best from the heart, soul, and mind, with all our strength! Giving our best is not about how much we give, how many ministries we're in, how good we think we are, or how fancy our church is. Because while man focuses on the quantity of a gift or service, God cares about the quality of the heart!

Do you ever stop in your tracks and ask yourself this key question; "Is what I'm doing pleasing to the Lord? Am I offering Him my best every day?" Because Jesus was the Son of God, of one nature with the Father, He knew what pleased God. But we are fallible human beings. How can we know what pleases Him? God has always made it clear to His people what it takes to please Him (Mic 6:8). "No, oh people, the Lord has told you what is good, and this is what He requires of you: to do what it is right, to love mercy and to walk humbly with your God."

We should know instinctively when we're doing wrong because we were created in the image of God (Gen 1:27)—and His laws are written in our hearts (Rom 2:15). When we choose against that inner knowledge of the indwelling Holy Spirit, we harden our hearts, and our consciences dry up. And eventually, we cannot tell good from evil (Rom 1:28).

But when we live by the Spirit in both our public and private lives, show mercy to those who wrong us, cling tightly to God's Word, and crave His presence, we will make choices that please Him. We will know and feel it through the presence of His Spirit in our daily life.

God was teaching the Israelites to give their best of the flocks and find the one animal without defect or blemish for the sacrifice. This wasn't easy because this animal was the cream of their crop, the most expensive, used for breeding, but it was what God demanded.

When we don't give our best to our Lord, we must question ourselves, have we indeed submitted our whole lives to Him with absolute trust and faith? Unfortunately, we have a half-hearted commitment to our Heavenly Father if we're not giving Him our highest standard at all levels.

When we are lacking in bringing God our foremost, we are only partially motivated to please Him, which means our offerings will always be inadequate. But believers who have genuinely tasted God's greatness and goodness will aim to offer the Father their supreme best for the rest of their lives! They will quit playing church and dedicate their all to true worship, committed to Him with their best "godly" interest at heart!

When we self-examine our lives and ensure that Jesus Christ is part of our evaluation, we will not want to give him our leftovers, second best, or what's in our reserve tank. We set our sights on providing him our best—and nothing less! The accurate indicator that we're giving the Lord our best is when His greatest commandment is alive in us, "Love the Lord with all of your heart, soul, mind and strength" (Luke 10:27). What does this mean?

'With all our hearts' implies that we wholly trust God's promises, wisdom, power, and love to help us in every circumstance. 'With all our soul' means that our spiritual appetite (hunger and thirst) is directed toward all of God's divine nature. It portrays how we live, the choices we make, and the behavior and lifestyle we embrace. 'With all our mind' means that all our thoughts and attitude are focused on Christlikeness. And 'with all our strength' means that all the spiritual strength within us is exercising the love of God daily and nothing else. This is accomplished by applying His word—with the guidance of the Holy Spirit.

It is so critical that we understand we're spiritually bankrupt without a Savior. Without the cleansing of sin that He provides and the empowering presence of the Holy Spirit who lives in the hearts of the redeemed, loving God to any degree is impossible. That is why His word reminds us that those who trust the Lord have hope and never need to fear difficulty or calamity. Why? Because they know Who is in control of their lives and that He is full of goodness.

Our love and affection for God should grow more intense as time passes during our sanctification stages as Christians. When we go through our most challenging times, fighting those fierce battles, and when we need Him the most, we should know that God was faithful and ever-present during those tough times. It should increase our faith, love, and strength with such deep compassion. And it should be evident in our daily witness to others what He has done in powerful ways.

Over time, we witness His compassion, mercy, grace, and love for each of us and His hatred for sin. This is important because He wants His righteous ones to show His holiness through all of life's ugliness. When God is our top priority, we're living out His word and the greatest commandment, demonstrating that we are in an all-out pursuit of His righteousness. It shows that we take His commands seriously: to love Him above all else. It exhibits that we are consumed with God's activities in life, and no matter what, we will offer Him our finest.

These types of Christians are eager to study and apply God's Word, pray, obey, and honor God in all things, and are willing and excited to share Jesus Christ with others. Through these spiritual disciplines, the love for God grows and matures, which glorifies and magnifies Him above all things in life!

Col 3:12–17, "Since God chose you to be the holy people he loves, you must clothe yourselves with tenderhearted mercy, kindness, humility, gentleness, and patience. Make allowance for each other's faults and forgive anyone who offends you. Remember, the Lord forgave you, so you must forgive others. Above all, clothe yourselves with love, which binds us all together in perfect harmony. And let the peace that comes from Christ rule in your hearts. For as members of one body, you are called to live in peace. And always be thankful and let the message about Christ, in all its richness, fill your lives. Teach and counsel each other with all the wisdom he gives. Sing Psalms and hymns and spiritual songs to God with thankful hearts. And whatever you do or say, do it as a representative of the Lord Jesus, giving thanks through him to God the Father."

CHAPTER 3

Genuine Compliance

Lev 3:1, "If you present an animal from the herd as a "peace of-fering to the LORD," it may be a male or a female, but it must have no defects." In each peace offering, the priest must present part of this offering as a special gift to the LORD, and when it was all in compliance with God's requirements, it was a pleasing aroma to the Lord."

When a person gave a peace offering, it expressed gratitude and established genuine fellowship with God. It symbolized peace, and here is a keynote; the person presenting it could eat part of the offering. This is a beautiful picture of God's physical and spiritual provision because His grace and goodness are present throughout the offering. And for us, genuine fellowship with our Lord is when He has our wholehearted commitment.

The peace offering was not an offering to make peace with God but to "enjoy peace with Him." The greatest peace offering happened when Jesus sac-rificed Himself on the cross. His sacrifice paid the penalty of our sin and made peace between the believer and God that can now be enjoyed. Paul tells us in Rom 5:1, "Therefore, since we have been made right in God's sight by faith, we have peace with God because of what Jesus Christ our Lord has done for us." Paul even notes in Ephesians 2:14–16 that Jesus Christ Himself has become our peace and has broken down the wall of separation. And when it comes to peace and fellowship with God, there is no male or female (Gal 3:28); "all are welcome before God."[1]

Fellowship with God is when we agree with Him in all things, and the New Testament assures believers of this partnership (1 Cor 1:9; 2 Cor 13:14;

1. Enduring Word Ministry, "The Peace Offering."

9

1 John 1:3). Today, there are considerable benefits in an authentic and proper fellowship with our Lord Jesus Christ. It's a friendship, companionship, and eternal bond that shows we're in unity with Him. Amos 3:3 reminds us, "Can two walk together unless they are agreed?" There must be like-mindedness at the heart of this relationship—because two in fellowship must have the exact wishes and desires—for they are always on the same page! There is never a disconnect; they are harmoniously and peacefully in sync.

Scripture identifies those things at odds that can jeopardize our true fellowship with God. They are the mind governed by the flesh that does not submit to God's law (Rom 8:7) and friendship with the ways of the world (Jas 4:4). We glorify our Lord by submitting to His will and obeying the commands in His word. Then, when immersed in His word, we will enjoy the harmony, contentment, and joy of God's fellowship.

A "genuine" walk and connection with the Lord will yield an experience of His absolute peace that many long for daily! What is the key to possessing that genuine fellowship with the Lord? The operative statement is when we follow His requirements, obediently committed to all His ways, and not just the ones that fit our comfort list!

David tells us in Psalms chapter thirty-seven to delight in the Lord and commit everything we have and do to Him! We can accomplish this by enjoying the experience of God's presence in our daily life, which can only happen by knowing Him better through His word. When we commit everything to our Lord, we entrust all we have into His Almighty Hands, believing in Him for all things. But when we fail to do this, we lack faith, which prevents us from knowing Him more and growing in the knowledge He provides us through His word.

When we comply with God, we seek Him daily for His counsel and guidance with a readiness and willingness to yield to His wishes and desires for our life, which is always for our good. A person complying with the Lord in all areas of their life is doing these things below:

- Dedicating and submitting their all to Him, Col 3:17.

- Willingness to surrender with complete humility, 1 Pet 5:5.

- Possesses a repentant heart, Joel 2:12–13.

- Will walk away from their old life to their new life in Christ, Eph 4:20–24.

- Has a genuine love for God's commands and all His ways, Deut 5:33.

- Has an accepting and cooperative attitude and will, Phil 2:3–5.

- Through it all, they are steadfast in their faith and trust in the Lord, 1 Pet 5:9–11

Ultimately, they're indulging more of the Lord in their life than the ways of the world.

> Zeph 2:1–3, "Gather together, yes, gather together, you shameless nation. Gather before judgment begins, before your time to repent is blown away like chaff. Act now before the fierce fury of the LORD falls and the terrible day of the LORD's anger begins. Seek the LORD, all who are humble, and follow his commands. Seek to do what is right and to live humbly.
>
> Perhaps even yet, the LORD will protect you, protect you from his anger on that day of destruction."

CHAPTER 4

Godly Discernment

Lev 4:1–3 "Then the LORD said to Moses, Give the following instructions to the people of Israel. This is how you are to deal with those who sin unintentionally by doing anything that violates one of the LORD's commands. If the high priest sins, bringing guilt upon the entire community, he must give a sin offering for the sin he has committed. He must present to the LORD a young bull with no defects."

A sin offering was one of two mandatory sacrifices in the Old Testament Law, which meant fault offering. It was to atone for any wrongdoing and cleanse unintentional or ignorant sins from defilement. This offering was sacrificed when a person sinned unintentionally by breaking one of the Lord's commandments and later realized his guilt (Lev 4:1–3, 4:27). Unintentional sin is related to transgressions that can result from straying away from God or by accident because of negligence. In these cases, a child of God could make an offering.

The author in Hebrews chapter two reminds us that we will stray away from God if we do not listen to His voice through His word, which can lead us to be blinded by those things we call the "little sins in life." It is hard to pay close attention to every little detail because it involves a complete focus on our minds, body, and hearts. And the key for us is when we listen to our Lord through the power of His word and Spirit; we must obey it to the detail.

Unfortunately, when we drift or wander away from God, it could be for various reasons:

- We're afraid that God may ask us to give up something dear to us.
- It could be a weak prayer life.
- There is a void in our genuine worship and fellowship with God.
- We're in the wrong community of people.
- Our pride is superseding godly humility.
- We're too distracted by the things of this world; we're spiritually imbalanced.
- We don't have enough patience.
- We lack complete faith in God.
- We have lost all sense of the knowledge of God's word.
- There is a sin in our life that has not been dealt with.

The Bible is clear; all have sinned and fallen short of God's glory, and we've all broken the Law of God whether or not we realize it; because humanity is sinful, and we are all guilty before God (Rom 3:23). Any sin can separate us from our Lord and create such a distance it will obscure our vision of what is right or wrong in our lives.

God's word reminds us in 2 Tim 3:16–17, "All Scripture is inspired by God and is useful to teach us what is true and to make us realize what is wrong in our lives. It corrects us when we are wrong and teaches us to do what is right. God uses it to prepare and equip his people to do every good work."

It must have been painful for sinners under the Mosaic Law to slaughter an innocent animal when they knew they were the ones who had done wrong. In the same way, it is painful for us to admit our guilt and to know that the innocent and holy Son of God took the punishment for our sins. Though every person has sinned (except Jesus), we have the opportunity for forgiveness and redemption from sin through the sacrifice of Jesus on the cross.

And the great news is this. By faith in Him, salvation is obtained (Eph 2:8–9). This is true regardless of intentional or unintentional sins, whether a person believes he has sinned a little or a lot. But in our ongoing battle against the enemy, the crucial question is this. Is our genuine insight and application of His wisdom and knowledge progressing in our maturity and sanctification stages? What is the status of our discerning spirit in these days of constant temptation?

Genuine spiritual discernment starts with prayer, for it is a gift bestowed by the Holy Spirit. A critical step in attaining this beautiful and so-needed gift is when a Christian applies spiritual wisdom, heeding God's word and listening to the Holy Spirit. That person will exhibit the characteristics of someone acting with godly wisdom and Christlikeness. Since Jesus is the model for living life, He showed us great examples of discernment. He emphasized not to seek the wisdom of the world because it clouds godly discernment.

That is why we must ingrain a Christlike conscience in our daily life because it helps us to hear God's voice and recognize the truth about God's ways and how we should live. It is a part of our God-given internal faculties and critical inner awareness that bears witness to the crazy norms of life. And another key takeaway is that it brings value and recognition when determining godly decisions. The conscience reacts when one's actions, thoughts, and words conform to—or are contrary to a standard of right and wrong.

As followers of Jesus Christ, we want to have a working conscience employed by the power of the Holy Spirit. The apostle Paul warned, "Now the Spirit expressly says that in latter times some will depart from the faith, giving heed to deceiving spirits and doctrines of demons, speaking lies in hypocrisy, having their own conscience seared with a hot iron" (1 Tim 4:1–2). As Christians in today's world of imbalanced godly principles, we must keep our consciences clear by obeying God and maintaining our relationship with Him in good standing. We do this by renewing, refreshing, and continually softening our hearts with His word.

God's word reminds us in Phil 1:9–11, "I pray that your love will overflow more and more and that you will keep on growing in knowledge and understanding. For I want you to understand what really matters, so that you may live pure and blameless lives until the day of Christ's return. May you always be filled with the fruit of your salvation, the righteous character produced in your life by Jesus Christ, for this will bring much glory and praise to God."

CHAPTER 5

Blinded Ignorance

Lev 5:17–19, "Suppose you sin by violating one of the LORD's commands. Even if you are unaware of what you have done, you are guilty and will be punished for your sin. For a guilt offering, you must bring to the priest your own ram with no defects, or you may buy one of equal value. Through this process, the priest will purify you from your unintentional sin, making you right with the LORD, and you will be forgiven. This is a guilt offering, for you have been guilty of an offense against the LORD." If someone desecrated the holy things of the Tabernacle, and was in this state of mind and said, "I didn't know," it was not an acceptable excuse. They still had to make a sacrifice to atone for their sin."

The guilt offering was used when someone had sinned regarding the holy things of God's dwelling place. When the sacred things of God were defiled, a mere sin offering was not enough; restitution was also required. If anyone treated the sacred things of the Tabernacle with disrespect and replied, "I didn't know," it was not an acceptable excuse.

Sins of ignorance differ from sins done with knowledge in the degree of guilt. Jesus said so in Luke 12:47–48: "And a servant who knows what the master wants, but isn't prepared and doesn't carry out those instructions, will be severely punished. But someone who does not know and then does something wrong will be punished only lightly." However, we must keep in mind that sin is sin! Big or small, knowing or unknowing—any sin can separate us from the will of God.

Jesus Christ has conveyed to us through His word how we're to live until His return. We must work diligently in obeying His commands daily and putting the scriptures into practice. And as believers, we've all been given enough gifts and responsibilities to keep us busy until He calls us to our Heavenly home. The more of an active Christian life we incorporate daily by utilizing all our God-given gifts, the less time we will have for acts of ignorant sins.

We can get trapped in these types of sins when we're not aware of what God's word is telling us, which can lead us to unfamiliar areas of our life that are not Christlike. This only happens when we're oblivious to the truth and knowledge of God's word—or ignore the convictions and guidance of the Holy Spirit. So, we need to ensure that we're experienced in the ways of God so we're not left unaware of His Truths! Charles Spurgeon once said, "Ignorance of the law of God is itself a breach of law since we are bidden to know and remember it." [1]

When you break down the definition of ignorance, it's simply the lack of knowledge or information about a topic. Ignorance occurs when we're unfamiliar, clueless, and inexperienced in an area of our life. And to compound it even more, when we're blinded to areas of spiritual weakness, it's because we lack perception, awareness, and discernment. When blinded ignorance is at its peak, we are entirely oblivious to the dangers of life that can affect us from a temporal condition, but most importantly to a permanent state.

The root cause of blinded ignorance is when we deprive ourselves of the complete understanding of something we desperately need daily. Because let's face it, we all need help in many ways to prevent us from failing in our spiritual walk. We cannot ignore this fundamental fact—in our constant spiritual battle, we will face many areas of the flesh where we will struggle. We all need to realize that the enemy is out to obscure our spiritual vision so he can lead us down a path of destruction—away from the glory of God. He snares us in three key areas; the pride of life, lust of the eyes, and lust of the flesh, which all come from this broken world (1 John 2:16). When the world consumes our lives over God, we're moving into areas of unfamiliar territories that can damage our faith and holiness.

When we get caught up in the realms of "consumed" secularism, we have cracked the foundation of our relationship with Christ because we are more fixated on more of the world than Him. The scary fact about secularism is **this—it's the** indifference to or "rejection or exclusion" of any religion and religious considerations. And this includes the one divine nature God wants more in our life: His holiness! When we deeply analyze our Christian life, we will discover that at the core of our blinded ignorance is a spiritual disease that is so debilitating, destructive, and disastrous, and that's "spiritual blindness."

1. Enduring Word Ministry, "The Trespass and Guilt Offering."

Spiritual Blindness is when we cannot see the word of God and experience the working of the Holy Spirit. It's as if we've completely shut out and shut down any working of God in our life. When Christians fall prey to this weakening defect, we find ourselves in the act of going against God and His ways (Rom 3:23).

Think about this. If we are going against something, we are separated from it. So, regardless of the size, big or small, any sin separates us from a Holy God. Spiritual blindness is a severe condition when someone cannot see Jesus Christ in their examination of life—and this leads to a lack of understanding and belief in "all of His teachings." And when people do not see Jesus Christ, they do not 'see' God (Col 1:15–16).

The primary cause of spiritual blindness is clear in God's word. "Satan, the god of this world, has blinded the minds of those who don't believe, so they cannot see the glorious light of the Good News. They don't understand this message about the glory of Christ, who is the exact likeness of God." (2 Cor 4:4). The enemy has been at work since man's fall, deceiving people any way he can from God's good purpose and plan. And today, he has intensified it even more because he does not want anyone to believe in Jesus Christ as the Savior of their life.

However, we have the Spirit of God reigning in our lives to ward off the debilitating effects of Satan's power and the world's influence (1 John 4:13). John tells us, "Whoever confesses that Jesus is the Son of God, God abides in Him, and he in God" (1 John 4:15). Satan wars within and outside of us—His weapons of internal and external warfare are deceitful and crafty schemes to make us doubt and stumble in our daily growth (2 Cor 2:11, Eph 4:14).

Remember, God has given us powerful weapons to fight off the enemy's flaming arrows (Ephesians 6:10-18). As believers, we can overcome evil by remaining in the one true Light so we will never become spiritually blind. For, in truth, Jesus has given us His tremendous promise in John 8:12, "Jesus spoke to the people once more and said, "I am the light of the world. If you follow me, you won't have to walk in darkness because you will have the light that leads to life." If we abide in His Light daily, we've discovered the antidote to spiritual blindness. [2]

2. Got Questions, "What Is Spiritual Blindness?"

CHAPTER 6

On Fire

> Lev 6:12–13, "Meanwhile, the fire on the altar must be kept burning; it must never go out. Each morning the priest will add fresh wood to the fire and arrange the burnt offering on it. He will then burn the fat of the peace offerings on it. Remember, the fire must be kept burning on the altar at all times. It must never go out."

The altar's fire was ignited miraculously from Heaven by God Himself (Lev 9:24), which added to why the altar's fire should never be allowed to be extinguished. This was *God's fire* and needed to be respected and cared for every second—of every minute—of every day. The fire of the altar should never go out, such as with our faith, love, and zeal for God in our daily lives. It's that flame of God He has given to indwell in us through the power of His Spirit (as believers), which should never fade or be covered up.

This continuously burning and divine fire helped to remind the Israelites of God's presence, His power, and their need for God. The long-burning character of the burnt offering is an appropriate illustration of the work of giving ourselves entirely to God. Coming to God as a living sacrifice is not quick work, and we may feel like, at times, that we, like the burnt offering, have endured the heat of the fire for a long time.[1] However, that fiery conviction is also there to purify and refine those critical areas in our life through our sanctification stages.

What does it take to keep the fire of the Lord burning within us? That faithful, loving, and bold compassion, as Solomon referred to in Song of Solomon 8:6–7? This perpetual burning fire within our spirit is crucial to our continual growth, refining, and shaping us daily. Because without it, we can be

---

1 Enduring Word Ministry, "Instructions for the Priests."

spiritually dull, if not spiritually dead. God is first identified as a "consuming fire" in Deut 4:24 and 9:3. God's holiness is the reason for His being a consuming fire. And always remember this. God's fire can burn up anything unholy.

Have we recognized those ungodly areas in our lives that are trying to put out God's consuming fire? What are we doing to feed His Holy blaze within us? We must keep fanning His flame and burn out those ways that are not pleasing to God. When we stand on His truth, trust it with all our heart and work to understand His teachings, we can learn how to apply them to our lives, possess a repentant heart, and submit ourselves wholeheartedly to His ways. It's then when our commitment will be more steadfast in keeping that fire aflame for His glory!

Here is a critical point. If we get complacent, start to slack, or ignore the word of God daily, the fire will begin to dim—but God will continue to try to get our attention. If we're distracted by other things, we will miss it and begin to loosen our grip unintentionally. Doubt is an evil tool that the enemy will use in our lives to dry up our flame— because he wants to blow out our holy fire!

Here is how we can keep the consuming fire of God ceaselessly generating within our lives:

- Adhere to the power of God's word daily! Hebrews 4:12–13

- Apply the biblical truth of His word in your life! Jas 1:22

- Access the power of the Holy Spirit in your life for Help! John 14:26, Rom 8:9

- Aspire to all His Truths in your daily life! 2 Tim 3:16–17

- Acquire an attitude of gratitude daily! 1 Thess 5:18

- Assure your closeness with the Lord through prayer! Jas 4:3, Phil 4:6, Eph 6:18

- Acknowledge your weak areas and ask for His strength! 2 Cor 12:9

- Armor yourself with the power of God against the enemy! Eph 6:10–17

- Admire the model of Christlikeness and embrace it! Phil 2:5, 1 John 2:6, 1 Cor 11:1, 1 Pet 2:21

- Accept God's will in your life, not yours! Ps 40:8, Matt 12:50, Jas 4:15

- Admit your sins with a heart of contrite and humility! 1 John 1:9, Ps 32:5, Ps 38:18

- Acclaim genuine Christlike worship and fellowship in your life! Heb 10:25, Matt 18:20, Ps 95:6–7, 1 Thess 5:11

- Ambitiously seek the Lord and all His holiness! Matt 6:33, 1 Chr 16:11

The constant fire in Leviticus chapter six was also connected to the idea that these sacrifices must be continually offered because of the perpetual sins of God's children. However, Jesus's perfect sacrifice on the cross was not a continual sacrifice; it was a once-for-all offering, as described in Heb 7:27, *"Unlike those other high priests, he does not need to offer sacrifices every day. They did this for their sins first and then for the sins of the people. But Jesus did this once and for all when he sacrificed himself for the people's sins."*

So often in our daily life, the fire of God goes out because of our drifting away from His word—and then we get caught up in the same old sinful acts. It's almost like we're crucifying our Savior on the cross repeatedly. An excellent guiding tool for Christians is in 1 Tim 6:11–14, "But you, Timothy, are a man of God; so, run from all these evil things. Pursue righteousness and a godly life, along with faith, love, perseverance, and gentleness. Fight the good fight for the true faith. Hold tightly to the eternal life to which God has called you, which you have declared so well before many witnesses. And I charge you before God, who gives life to all, and before Christ Jesus, who gave a good testimony before Pontius Pilate, that you obey this command without wavering. Then no one can find fault with you from now until our Lord Jesus Christ comes again."

As Christians, the best way we can signify that the consuming fire of God is alive and at work in us is when we are actively pursuing, fighting, and holding tightly to our faith in Jesus Christ and by obeying Him in all His ways. No, it is not easy. But that fire of God has been lit up inside of you and me for a reason and purpose.

That fire is at its full use and power when we're in His word, applying it to our daily life and yielding to the power of the Holy Spirit for guidance. Just like a physical fire lit under us would make us get up and flee—the same action should apply to us spiritually. God's fire is seen in and through us "when we get up and get going for the cause of Christ!"

Rom 1:16–17, "For I am not ashamed of this Good News about Christ. It is the power of God at work, saving everyone who believes—the Jew first and also the Gentile. This Good News tells us how God makes us right in his sight. This is accomplished from start to finish by faith. As the Scriptures say, "It is through faith that a righteous person has life."

CHAPTER 7

The Light

Lev 7:19–21, "Meat that touches anything ceremonially unclean may not be eaten; it must be completely burned up. The rest of the meat may be eaten, but only by people who are ceremonially clean. If you are ceremonially unclean and you eat meat from a peace offering that was presented to the LORD, you will be cut off from the community. If you touch anything that is unclean (whether it is human defilement or an unclean animal or any other unclean, detestable thing) and then eat meat from a peace offering presented to the LORD, you will be cut off from the community."

In this chapter, God further instructed the guilt and peace offerings. It always seemed God had to provide additional instructions for His children because the Israelites needed to understand this crucial point, and it was this; to receive God's blessings of forgiveness through these sacrifices, *they must comply with His detailed guidelines.* But they would also know that these instructions were of God, not man. They would realize He was in control of everything.

The importance of each offering and the main reason for further instructions were 1) to prepare them for the Glory of God, 2) to illustrate God's holiness, 3) to reveal people's sinfulness, 4) to demonstrate devotion to God, and thankfulness to Him, 5) to cleanse their sins and symbolize the repentance of the sinner, 6) to show God's mercy and His atonement, 7) to establish obedience and faith in God, 8) to gain God's acceptance 9) enabled the sinner to approach a Holy God, and 10) to show them that everything belonged to God, first!

Ceremonial purity was required of anyone who wanted to participate in the fellowship meal associated with the peace offering. *This illustrates the principle that we cannot enjoy the peace of God until we have received His cleansing grace.* It was a grave sin if a ceremonially unclean person ate the meat of a peace offering. Such disregard for the holiness of God's sacrifice meant that a person should be cut off from his people. Presumably, the decisive penalty of ex-communication was reserved for those who *knowingly* ate the peace offering while unclean. If they did it accidentally or unknowingly, a sacrifice was accepted explicitly for it (Lev 5:2).[2]

Today, God does not need to give us further instructions. We should know by now what is acceptable or unacceptable, pure or impure, clean or unclean, right or wrong, and the difference between darkness and Light. The author in Hebrews chapter six reminds mature Christians to stop going over the basics of Christianity. Let us go on instead and become mature in our understanding. And Peter reminds us in His second epistle that God has already given us every resource for living a godly life. It is designed to help develop, promote, and progress His divine nature.

These specific directions are a blessing for us today. Why? He knows the plans He has for you and me. Jeremiah 29:11–13 reminds us, *"For I know the plans I have for you," says the Lord. "They are plans for good and not for disaster, to give you a future and a hope. In those days when you pray, I will listen. If you look for me wholeheartedly, you will find me."*

The key to this passage is: "If we look for Him wholeheartedly." And the only way we can rest in that blessed assurance is to live in His Light daily. This Light is our guide and represents all that is good, pure, genuine, righteous, and holy. It is the only source for leading us in a manner that honors God. If we're not living in the Light of His Truth, darkness will prevail, and it can cut us off from the family of God.

God's word tells us in 2 John 3:6–8, *"Anyone who continues to live in him will not sin. But anyone who keeps sinning does not know him or understand who he is. Dear children, don't let anyone deceive you about this: When people do what is right, it shows they are righteous, even as Christ is righteous. But when people keep sinning, it shows they belong to the devil, who has sinned since the beginning. But the Son of God came to destroy the works of the devil."*

The only way to have an ongoing relationship with our Lord is to distinguish and put aside all sinful ways of living, which means all sins! If not, our Lord will expose them and judge all deceit accordingly. In the Old Testament, believers symbolically transferred their iniquities to animals based on God's specifications. The animal died in that sinners' place, and they could continue to live in God's favor. He would graciously forgive them because of their faith.

---

2. Enduring Word Ministry, "Gifts of the Twelve Tribes."

When Jesus Christ came to this Earth (God in the flesh), He came to die once and for all the sins of the world; for those who place their faith and trust in what He did. He paid our penalty on that cross, and the only way we can be identified with Him is when we accept His sacrifice, nail our sinful desires to the cross, and live our new life in Christ. And this is symbolic of our Risen Savior. However, the Light and the dark cannot coexist, so the choice comes down to us individually.

And when we choose to walk in the Light, we can walk with confidence and boldness, knowing that Jesus, the Light of the world, is leading our way by His Spirit. John 8:12 Jesus spoke to the people once more and said, *"I am the light of the world. If you follow me, you won't have to walk in darkness because you will have the light that leads to life."*

When people get lost in spiritual darkness, they live apart from God and need further instructions on how to get back to Him. However, no matter how deep the darkness, the light of God's love and truth overcomes every sin that separates us from God, and only when we surrender and submit to Him can we be led back to His cleansing grace!

> 1 John 1:6–10, *"This is the message we heard from Jesus and now declare to you: God is light, and there is no darkness in him at all. So, we are lying if we say we have fellowship with God but go on living in spiritual darkness; we are not practicing the truth. But if we are living in the light, as God is in the light, then we have fellowship with each other, and the blood of Jesus, his Son, cleanses us from all sin. If we claim we have no sin, we are only fooling ourselves and not living in the truth. But if we confess our sins to him, he is faithful, forgives us, and cleanses us from all wickedness. If we claim we have not sinned, we are calling God a liar and showing that his word has no place in our hearts."*

Because of what Christ did for you and me on the cross, when God looks at the cross—He sees you and me. And when He looks at us, He sees His Son, Jesus Christ. Wow! Think about the power of that statement (Eph 1:3–14, 2 Cor 5:21). Is the power of that Light visible in our daily life?

CHAPTER 8

Public Christians

Lev 8:1–6, "Then the LORD said to Moses, "Bring Aaron and his sons, along with their sacred garments, the anointing oil, the bull for the sin offering, the two rams, and the basket of bread made without yeast, and call the entire community of Israel together at the entrance of the Tabernacle. So, Moses followed the LORD's instructions, and the whole community assembled at the Tabernacle entrance. Moses said, "This is what the LORD has commanded us to do!" Then he presented Aaron and his sons and washed them with water."

Only the descendants of Aaron could be priests. They had the distinct honor and responsibility of performing sacrifices. Nevertheless, as the special tribe of Levi, they had to be cleansed and set apart for the work of God! They had to dedicate themselves according to God's specifications before they could help the people do the same. They would be washed with water, clothed with special garments, and anointed with oil. God's guidelines for this ceremony showed that holiness came from God alone, not man's rituals.

Why were these priests needed? Ever since the fall of man, there's been a gap between man and God because of their sinful nature, and people needed a mediator to help them find forgiveness. At one time, the Patriarchs were priests and sacrificed for the family. But when God's children left Egypt, the descendants of Aaron were chosen to serve as priests of the nation of Israel. They were appointed to stand in the gap between God and man.

This was their full-time position, and they were the overseers of the offerings. They had a high calling from Almighty God and had to be the godly example for His children, which was the importance of this ordination being conducted publicly, not secretly! And they were utterly devoted to the call of God!

The process of consecration began with cleansing, which was humbling because it took place openly at the door of the Tabernacle of the meeting. What a beautiful depiction for us today. We cannot be cleansed of our sins without being humbled first. And God, in all His divine ways, shows us in this illustration the parallel of His word in Matt 10:32, "Everyone who acknowledges me publicly here on earth, I will also acknowledge before my Father in heaven."

The confession of Jesus Christ as Lord and Savior of our lives is necessary for every believer. It is not enough to believe in Him with our heart, but a confession must also be made with the mouth, which lies in accrediting their salvation to Him as Lord. Rom 10:9–11 reminds us, "If you openly declare that Jesus is Lord and believe in your heart that God raised him from the dead, you will be saved. For it is by believing in your heart that you are made right with God, and it is by openly declaring your faith that you are saved. As the Scriptures tell us, "Anyone who trusts in him will never be disgraced."

When we declare our faith in Christ to others and share with them what He has done in our lives, we're proclaiming that we're subjecting our lives to His ways and joining in fellowship with His body of believers. As a result, our new life starts to develop Christlike words and deeds visible in our homes, workplaces, churches, streets, and everywhere we go. It's a sincere commitment to change so the world knows Who oversees our life.

Like these old priests, dedicating their services to God, when we commit our lives to Jesus Christ as Lord, we must come to Him in humility and be willing to follow all His ways publicly. This leads me to pose a question. Is it ok to live a Christian life secretly? In other words, is it ok to keep our faith in Jesus Christ to ourselves? We need to read the entire context of what Jesus is saying not only in Matt 10:32 but also in the scriptures, from verse sixteen throughout its duration to the end of this chapter. The power of Jesus' message to His disciples lies in preparation for persecution.

So, that leads us to Jesus' profound message in Matt 10:34–42 when He makes it clear that "He did not come to bring peace but a sword, He came to divide" (Matt 10:32–34). Christ tells us, "If the world hates you, remember that it hated me first. The world would love you as one of its own if you belonged to it, but you are no longer part of the world. I chose you to come out of the world, so it hates you." (John 15:18–19). While it is understandable for someone to keep their faith in Christ a secret to save their life, it is vitally important that we clearly understand that for a Christian, a secret faith is not an option for true believers.

Our purpose on Earth is to be the light of the world and the salt of the earth, telling others the wonderful life-saving news of Jesus Christ and what He's done in our lives. Yes, sometimes we risk persecution and sometimes our own life. But we know it is God's will that we share His truth with others. And we also know He is powerful enough to protect us until our mission on Earth is completed. He did not create us for a life of complacency in the flesh. But an eternal, destined life that is content in proclaiming His truth to anyone and everyone around us.

There is only one way to show our proper identification as dedicated Christians. And that's by physically, verbally, and spiritually letting the world see Who is truly Lord of our lives. Living for Christ in this world can be difficult, but we all know that this world is not our home because it is a wicked battlefield.

The trials of our life are the tools God uses to build us up and make us more like His Son, Jesus Christ. In those trying times, we look to Christ and yield to the Holy Spirit so He can work within us. Just before His ascension into Heaven, Jesus gave us some of His most powerful and final words of authority regarding how we are charged to spread the gospel to the world (the Great Commission)—and this can only be accomplished publicly!

His final command and promise in Matt 28:20 tells us, "Teach these new disciples to obey all the commands I have given you. And be sure of this: I am with you always, even to the end of the age". And for you and me today, nothing else matters because these are our marching orders. We should exercise it to all extremes so our Lord knows we took His last order of work and command to heart.

As believers, our Mediator is Jesus Christ. Nothing you or I can do on our own would be sufficient to mediate between ourselves and God. No amount of good works or law-keeping makes us righteous enough to stand before a holy God (Isa 64:6; Rom 3:20; Gal 2:16). Without a Mediator, we are destined to spend eternity in hell, for by ourselves, salvation from our sin is impossible. Yet there is hope! "For there is one God and one Mediator between God and humans, and that is the man Christ Jesus" (1 Tim 2:5). Jesus represents those who have placed their absolute trust in Him.

As a defense attorney does for his client, he mediates for that person, telling the judge, "Your honor, my client is innocent of all charges,"—and that mediator goes to all extremes to show and prove to the judge why we are innocent. Some day we will face God, but we will do so as forgiven sinners because of Jesus' death on our behalf. Our "Defense Attorney and Mediator" (Christ) took the penalty for you and me, but we must give Him good reason and cause to defend our case to the Judge (God) as His dedicated servants! Will our case and cause for Christ be grounds for dismissal or approval?

As His Citizens of Heaven on this Earth and accountable Christians, we should be longing to hear those beautiful words, "Well done, my good and faithful servant." We cannot be a public Christian until we've died to self, taking on Christlike humility and trusting in the Lord for all things in our daily life, and not ourselves.

If the evil ones of this world do not hate us and they still accept us as their friends, could it be that we're too silent about our genuine faith in Christ? Are we being too discreet and covering up our real identity in Jesus so that we can be accepted by those not even part of God's family?

> 2 Tim 2:15–19, "Work hard so you can present yourself to God and receive his approval. Be a good worker, one who does not need to be ashamed and who correctly explains the word of truth. Avoid worthless, foolish talk that only leads to more godless behavior. This kind of talk spreads like cancer, as in the case of Hymenaeus and Philetus. They have left the path of truth, claiming that the resurrection of the dead has already occurred; in this way, they have turned some people away from the faith." But God's truth stands firm like a foundation stone with this inscription: "The LORD knows those who are his," and "All who belong to the LORD must turn away from evil."

CHAPTER 9

Starting Point

Lev 9:4–6, 22–24 "Present all these offerings to the LORD because the LORD will appear to you today. So, the people presented all these things at the entrance of the Tabernacle, just as Moses had commanded. Then the whole community came forward and stood before the LORD. And Moses said, "This is what the LORD has commanded you to do so that the glory of the LORD may appear to you" … "After that, Aaron raised his hands toward the people and blessed them. Then, after presenting the sin offering, the burnt offering, and the peace offering, he stepped down from the altar. Then Moses and Aaron went into the Tabernacle, and when they came back out, they blessed the people again, and the glory of the LORD appeared to the whole community. Fire blazed forth from the LORD's presence and consumed the burnt offering and the fat on the altar. When the people saw this, they shouted with joy and fell face down on the ground."

The theme of Leviticus chapter nine is "The Priests Begin Their Work." After all the preparation of each offering by "God's specific instructions," *only then would the glory of the Lord appear.* That was the importance of God's further instructions for the priests in preparing the Israelites for God's glory because the *"separation of unholiness"* would open the door to His glorious presence.

The priests did not have a day's rest from their services unto the Lord. Their work was constant, and everyday duties were required of God. *Therefore, they would give up their account of other things in life with joy to serve their responsibility to God and the community.* On this day, their objective was that the preparation, at the Lord's request, would be ready and on display for His glory!

Once we give our lives to Jesus Christ, the starting point of the presence of the Holy Spirit is with us, ready to begin His work in each believer until its completion. But what's missing in so many believers today is the absolute knowledge and keen sense that He's with us from beginning to end. I firmly believe that if every Christ-follower recognized God's presence in their daily life, they would be more in tune with their spiritual gifts and ready to put them to work with joy, just like the Levi Priests.

After all, Our Heavenly Father created us in His image. He offers us the best advice that prevents us from doing more damage to ourselves. He wants the best for us because He loves us! God knows we will never be perfect, but He wants us to strive for His holiness and model our lives after His Son, the High Priest, Jesus Christ. His open door for you and me is when we separate our lives from the world and unto His service.

But we will only be aware of His presence in our daily lives once we heed His advice and guidelines. A keen understanding of someone's presence is vital to any relationship, especially the one we have with God. While being aware of Him ensures nothing, failing to recognize His presence can ensure many adverse outcomes that could be detrimental. That's why our connection with Him is so important. Therefore, we must cling to His vital elements to sustain our spiritual living for today.

The only way we can know God's glorious presence in our lives is when 1) we're continually thinking about Him, 2) we're meditating on His word daily and applying it to our lives, 3) we're constantly seeking Him and His counsel, 4) we're separating ourselves from the ways of the world, 5) we're diligently praying to Him, 6) we're fervently walking with Him, 7) we're consistently thanking Him, 8) we receive and accept His will and plans for our life, 9) we're yearning to worship and praise Him more, and 10) we're focused on pleasing Him.

When we feel and know that His presence is amongst us, it makes a massive difference in how we look at ourselves, others, and the world. It solidifies our faith, hope, and Christlike love. It strengthens us to endure and persevere through life's difficulties and allows us to share the Good News with others. It powerfully preps us for the next phase of our serving Him! And the mightiness of that connection is confirmed through the power of His Holy Spirit. We will surely know God's presence when we're consumed with this type of heart and mindset. And the great news; it will lead us to a willingness to start new areas of service for our Lord with complete joy!

Our daily Christian walk is more than life; it's by His word and Holy Spirit and our continual sanctification that guides every aspect of our lives in word and deed. Throughout the Bible, we are commanded to love and serve

God with all our heart, soul, mind, and strength. And when we do, it will always yield a good return. Like the Priests, we should be diligent and faithful to remain in God's service our entire lives.

We are promised throughout Scripture that God will not abandon us, and one way this proves true is that He will always bring about a result when His Word is preached. So, our part is to remain steady in our service, and if we remain faithful to His will, we can see the elements of His plans unfold in our lives. And what a wonderful blanket of security and comfort we can have as we start our service for Him with joy. Because joy is one component that brings awareness of God's presence in our life! Remember, "The joy of the Lord is my strength," Neh 8:10.

> 1 Cor 15:58, "So, my dear brothers and sisters, be strong and immovable. Always work enthusiastically for the Lord, for you know that nothing you do for the Lord is ever useless."

> Phil 1:6, "And I am certain that God, who began the good work within you, will continue his work until it is finally finished on the day when Christ Jesus returns."

CHAPTER 10

Careless Spirits

> Lev 10:1–3, "Aaron's sons Nadab and Abihu put coals of fire in their incense burners and sprinkled incense over them. In this way, they disobeyed the LORD by burning before him the wrong kind of fire, different than he had commanded. So, fire blazed forth from the LORD's presence and burned them up, and they died there before the LORD. Then Moses said to Aaron, "This is what the LORD meant when he said, 'I will display my holiness through those who come near me. I will display my glory before all the people.' And Aaron was silent."

Aaron's sons were careless and irresponsible about following the specific laws and instructions for sacrifices. And in response to their disobedience, God destroyed them with a blast of fire. God's detailed instructions were set forth to establish deep respect and obedience to Him; if not, there would be repercussions.

God always has a good reason for His specific commands because His ways are always the best for us! However, there will always be consequences if we consciously or carelessly disobey His word. They died by fire because it was by fire that they sinned. When we disobey God, it's like *saying His word is not essential to our lives.* He reminds us, oh so well, that if we love Him, we will keep His commandments (John 14:15).

Aaron's sons grew up with the knowledge of God. They witnessed incredible miracles and possessed a legacy of great spiritual experiences. Not sure what their motivation was that led them to disobey God's guidelines. It could have been pride, self-ambition, or lack of patience, because they may have thought the ongoing seven-day sacrifice was too tedious. Regardless, this shows that a legacy of spiritual experiences cannot make us right with God. But an abiding relationship through complete obedience to the commands of His word will.

The fire on the altar of burnt offerings was sacred because it was kindled by God Himself (Lev 9:24), but Nadab and Abihu offered a fire of their own making. Perhaps they thought all fire was the same, and an undiscerning person would agree. But all fire isn't the same because there is a vast difference between the fire kindled by God and a fire conjured up by man. [1]

Disobedience can have consequences for us and others near us, such as with Aaron's sons. It is the underlying tone of 3 Bad C's: 1) No *Connection* with the Lord, 2) No *Communion* with His Spirit, 3) and No *Concern* about the outcome. And the culmination of these three components is because of a careless spirit.

However, the counter to this ill effect is 1) A godly heart set (Jer 17:9–10, Ezek 36:26–27, 2 Cor 5:17), 2) Controlling our minds (2 Cor 10:5, Rom 8:5–8), and 3) Submitting ourselves humbly to Him (Jas 4:7–10 and 1 Pet 5:6). We can't afford to drift away from God—but in return, run and draw near to Him!

We may not think carelessness is a major sin, but it is. According to the New Testament, carelessness can hinder one from going with the Lord when He appears. A negative characteristic of carelessness falls into the category of foolishness and is the unwillingness to think ahead. In many cases, they are more reactive to a blindside than being spiritually proactive. Careless spirits can be unsafe, reckless, mindless, negligent, and unguarded. These are all areas of spiritual hazard!

However, the opposite of a careless spirit is one who is cautious, vigilant, safe, alert, watchful, and proactive. God's word reminds us in Prov 22:3, "A prudent person foresees danger and takes precautions." The simpleton goes blindly on and suffers the consequences." Please look at some powerful examples of proactive planning in the two scriptures below. This clearly shows us that we must prepare spiritually with God's word and allow the Holy Spirit to lead us. Thinking ahead is putting ourselves in the future and deciding if our present behavior will cause us to be joyful or anguished in the coming days.

Matt 25:1–4, *"Then the Kingdom of Heaven will be like ten bridesmaids who took their lamps and went to meet the bridegroom. Five of them were foolish, and five were wise. The five who were foolish didn't take enough olive oil for their lamps, but the other five were wise enough to take along extra oil."*

Heb 2:1, *"So we must listen very carefully to the truth we have heard, or we may drift away from it."*

---

1. Enduring Word Ministry, "The Conduct of Priests."

Each one of us is responsible for the state of our spiritual condition. When we get careless in our Christian life, it can refer to a lack of awareness of a specific behavior that needs to be addressed and most times; it's when we neglect to nurture a weak spiritual area. It is usually because of a lack of concern or inattentiveness, and that's because of spiritual blindness. And the key to this is exercising our faith, which is not about quantity but quality. God's word reminds us in Luke 17:5–6 *that faith can be as small as a mustard seed.* Always remember this—just a tiny bit of faith in God can move any mountain!

We must ensure that our spiritual censers are lit by God's fire, not man's. Because when we get careless with the ways of the world, it can lead to dire consequences. In today's culture, if we lack watchfulness or attentiveness, that's a powerful indicator that we don't believe the threat is imminent, which is a dangerous mindset. So, we must always be discerning, wise, strong, and "stand firm in the faith."

A good example is the story of Aaron's sons. Their standards and lack of attention to God's guidelines led to their death. Getting too complacent, soft, timid, lazy, and weak in nurturing our spiritual life can lead to careless thoughts and actions. However, a caring godly spirit exhibits a strong positive regard for their Christlike character and genuine affection for others. It's no longer about ourselves but about God first, then others.

Isa 30:21, *"Your own ears will hear him. Right behind you, a voice will say, "This is the way you should go," whether to the right or to the left."* When the people of Jerusalem left God's path, He corrected them. He will do the same for us today if our ears hear His voice and act willingly and faithfully.

CHAPTER 11

Unclean Habits

Lev 11:8, "You may not eat the meat of these animals or even touch
their carcasses. They are ceremonially unclean for you." Not fit!

God strictly forbade eating unclean or impure meat in this simple short passage. He did not even want them touching it, for it represented unholiness.
The people would not be worthy of being in His presence because to be present before a Holy God, their worship had to be of purity and separate from
any corruption.

In all these strict dietary laws, you can see that God wanted His children
to demonstrate complete obedience to Him. They needed to separate themselves from the practices of the pagan people because His requirements were
the best for them physically and spiritually. God is specific in His marching
orders for those who want to serve and follow Him, and it always hinges upon
how we respond.

Just like then, God must keep providing His children with further instructions. Why? Because most people do not realize how the enemy is at
work using our little unclean thoughts and habits to begin his manifestation of
evil in our lives. A thought is only an idea, but if we dwell upon it long enough,
it becomes a habitual action. And then we've allowed that tempting thought to
consume our flesh, which will lead us to sin.

The main reason why our nation is filled with so much violence, and
uncleanness is because society has chosen to respond with self-indulgence.
They want to be fed by the enemy's spoon, not God's. And this wicked and
thought-provoked life can and will separate anyone from a Holy God. These
tiny seeds of temptation have now blossomed into the fruit of evil, leading to
the battle vs. the Spirit! And when people dabble with small tastes of sin, they

will be trapped by its sinful and unclean ways of life—sooner or later! But are they even aware of it?

That's why true and genuine worship is imperative in our daily walk with the Lord because it's the acknowledgment of God's ways and all His power at work in everything we do. Worship is not a once-a-week event. It's perpetual because it simply means the constant feeling or expression of reverence and adoration to Him, showing high regard for His ways.

When we incorporate this in our daily lives, it 1) renews our minds and hearts, 2) realigns us with the word of God, 3) restores our strength in Him, 4) refreshes and revives our soul, and 5) refuels our spirit, which ignites our joy and peace in ways we cannot fathom. And when we're in tune with a Holy God, we see the work of the Holy Spirit, Who is accessible and can enable us to walk in all His truths! And this assures us that our Lord is fighting our battles and helping us to endure and persevere through life.

At the core of this is a crucial element, which is motivation. It is a determined ambition driven by enthusiasm to behave in a particular way, with reason and purpose! The by-products of a genuinely motivated person dedicated to the Lord will result in absolute loyalty and admiration to Him alone! We must always remember that true worship is not limited to one act but is done correctly when the heart and attitude of the person are in the right spiritual place. And that right place is this, "You're responding to Him in all His ways of righteousness and holiness!"

No doubt, for so many, the pressures of today's life make it easy to ignore or forget our godly path. God reminds us in His scripture that He has already provided us with everything we need to live a godly life. And that's why we must avoid repeating those little errs in life. As noted earlier, we live in a culture filled with depraved minds and hearts that led to this sin-induced society.

We will all struggle with temptations at one point because it's inevitable. But here's the good news—God shows us a way out and will help us resist those weak areas (1 Cor 10:13). The vital point is to regularly study and apply God's word in every area of our lives. This will remind us why God wants us to live a life of purity and holiness. It keeps us connected with Him daily because those little things of the world can creep in and take over.

While some habits may be innocent and just fun, we must remind ourselves that habits become very serious regarding spiritual matters. Why? Because our flesh is so weak, we eventually succumb to those sinful habits. Such as losing our temper, our money toys, failing to control our tongue, more about self than others, taking part in pagan events (yes, even today), and drinking that leads to disorientation or drunkenness.

When we partake in unholy events ahead of worshipping God, it will lead to more gluttony, worrying, gossiping, entertaining lustful thoughts, coveting, and jealousy. And, of course, addiction to drugs, alcohol, gambling, TV, video games, a consuming world of secularism, etc. Any repeated attitude or action that dishonors God and supersedes honoring Him first is a sinful habit. And these can be very hard to break and detrimental to our daily walk with the Lord if we continue to live in their deadly pleasures. (1 Cor 6:9)

> Gal 5:16–25, "So I say, let the Holy Spirit guide your lives. Then you won't be doing what your sinful nature craves. The sinful nature wants to do evil, which is just the opposite of what the Spirit wants. And the Spirit gives us desires that are the opposite of what the sinful nature desires. These two forces are constantly fighting each other, so you are not free to carry out your good intentions. But when you are directed by the Spirit, you are not under obligation to the law of Moses. When you follow the desires of your sinful nature, the results are very clear: sexual immorality, impurity, lustful pleasures, idolatry, sorcery, hostility, quarreling, jealousy, outbursts of anger, selfish ambition, dissension, division, envy, drunkenness, wild parties, and other sins like these. Let me tell you again, as I have before, that anyone living that sort of life will not inherit the Kingdom of God."

> "But the Holy Spirit produces this kind of fruit in our lives: love, joy, peace, patience, kindness, goodness, faithfulness, gentleness, and self-control. There is no law against these things! Those who belong to Christ Jesus have nailed the passions and desires of their sinful nature to his cross and crucified them there. Since we are living by the Spirit, let us follow the Spirit's leading in every part of our lives. Let us not become conceited, or provoke one another, or be jealous of one another."

CHAPTER 12

Spiritual Purification

Lev 12:4, "The LORD said to Moses, "Give the following instructions to the people of Israel. If a woman becomes pregnant and gives birth to a son, she will be ceremonially unclean for seven days, just as she is unclean during her menstrual period. On the eighth day, the boy's foreskin must be circumcised. After waiting thirty-three days, she will be purified from the bleeding of childbirth. During this time of purification, she must not touch anything that is set apart as holy. And she must not enter the sanctuary until her time of purification is over."

Circumcision was not unknown in the ancient world; it was a ritual practice among various people. Yet for the Israelites, God's chosen children, circumcision was vital because it was the sign of the covenant between God and man. God created a covenant with Abraham, who, in turn, passed this covenant down to his descendants. Circumcision was added to this covenant as a symbol of man's devotion to God and their willingness to follow His commandments. But more importantly, circumcision is a cutting away of the flesh and an appropriate sign of the covenant for those who should put no trust in the flesh but in God!

In the Bible, circumcision almost always refers to a physical act, which is also true in Paul's writings. But in at least three passages, he alludes to a circumcision of the heart, which is a spiritual circumcision. Rom 2:28–29, Phil 3:3, and Col 2:11 discusses this initiation. Rather than cutting off a small part of the flesh, it is a cutting from the fleshly nature.

During purification, God clearly instructs the woman that she cannot touch anything holy. The key to understanding this ceremony is to comprehend the idea of original sin. As wonderful as a new baby is, God wanted it to be remembered that another sinner was brought into the world with every birth. In this symbolic picture, the mother was responsible for bringing a new sinner into the world. The trace of imperfection and sin was attached to every child as they came into this world, and this fact of humanity cannot be escaped. That's why there must be a stage of purification.[1]

Purification is the act of removing harmful substances from something. In the Bible, it's the act of drawing from a person, usually by a ceremony, the harmful effects they suffer because they have broken a religious or moral law. Purity is freedom from anything that contaminates and is the quality of being faultless, uncompromised, or unadulterated, just like pure water is free from other substances. And, like pure gold, which has been refined to such a degree that all debris and trash have been removed. A believer striving for a life of God's holiness is one in which sin no longer determines their choices in everyday life because they know the difference between what's pure in God's sight and what's not.

Is the state of purity important to God? Absolutely! Because in the scriptures, it's communicated as a means of perfection or holiness, which is an essential nature of God's divine being. And here is the key. When we have been born again through faith in Jesus (John 3:3), we pursue His righteousness and ways of holy living with the desire to live in purity (1 Pet 1:15–16). Like second nature, purity should define our thoughts, words, and actions. Jesus said, "Blessed are the pure in heart, for they shall see God" (Matt 5:8).

When our hearts are clouded with impurities, we cannot experience God's presence or hear His voice of clarity and truth. But when our claim to righteousness is based on what Jesus has done (Titus 3:5), we will strive to forsake sin (1 John 3:9) and live in purity of heart, enjoying fellowship with the God of holiness.

We must chase after Righteousness because it is the condition of being proven or declared morally excellent, while holiness is the condition of being consecrated or dedicated to moral excellence. Think of it this way: A ballerina who dances for the New York City Ballet has been declared good enough to be part of that company. From a young age, she has set herself apart for that purpose. While honing her skills, she continues to practice and improve as she dances.

In this analogy, righteousness is the ballerina's position in the ballet company. She has been given a job, her talents have been approved, and she belongs to the company. Holiness is the ballerina's dedication and devotion to her art. Everything in her life, what she eats, whom she knows, and how she spends her time and money, bows to this purpose.[2]

---

1. Enduring Word Ministry, "Cleansing after Childbirth."
2. Got Questions, "What Is the Difference?"

Practicing godly righteousness means having the courage to maintain our Christlike integrity, honesty, and values regardless of the circumstance. It's rejecting the vices of the ungodly and all falsehoods and aligning ourselves with the words and actions of Jesus Christ towards everyone, regardless. Our standard of conduct and behaviors should be in order with the ways of our Holy God and not the ways of an unholy world.

When our Christian lives have been circumcised from the ways of the world, and we've been spiritually purified inside and out, we've been cleansed of the world's impurities. We can now pursue the Righteous One with an eagerness and willingness that is refreshing and rewarding. God's word reminds us in Ps 11:7 that our Lord is Righteous, and He loves those who live righteously, for they will see His face!

We are responsible for the well-being of something significant to the body of Christ, and that's the condition of our Christlike heart, which is vital to holiness. Jesus Christ even teaches us the importance of this inner purity in the fifteenth chapter of Matthew. This great analogy shows us that we can quickly focus on the attractiveness of our outer selves but disregard an essential part our Lord is most concerned about: Our inner being—mainly our heart.

A faithful follower of Jesus Christ is changed on the inside to that state of purity (not perfection), and it's reflected on the outside in a manner that's pleasing to God. This process will continue to change us if we comply with His guidelines and allow the Holy Spirit to establish healthy thoughts, motives, and actions.

Matt 15:16–20, "Don't you understand yet?" Jesus asked. "Anything you eat passes through the stomach and then goes into the sewer. But the words you speak come from the heart; that's what defiles you. For from the heart come evil thoughts, murder, adultery, all sexual immorality, theft, lying, and slander. These are what defile you. Eating with unwashed hands will never defile you."

A pure heart has no hypocrisy or hidden motives; they have a heart toward God. It is transparent and has a willing & yearning desire to please God in all areas of their life. It is more than an external purity of behavior; it is an internal purity of the soul. 2 Tim 2:21–22, "If you keep yourself pure, you will be a special utensil for honorable use. Your life will be clean, and you will be ready for the Master to use you for every good work." Like the old priests, we must attain and maintain that purity today.

Person, Utilizing, Righteousness, Everyday!

CHAPTER 13

Contagious Sins

Lev 13:9–13, "Anyone who develops a serious skin disease must go to the priest for an examination. If the priest finds a white swelling on the skin, some hair on the spot has turned white, and there is an open sore in the affected area, it is a chronic skin disease, and the priest must pronounce the person ceremonially unclean. In such cases, the person need not be quarantined, for it is obvious that the skin is defiled by the disease. Now suppose the disease has spread all over the person's skin, covering the body from head to foot. When the priest examines the infected person and finds that the disease covers the entire body, he will pronounce the person ceremonially clean. Since the skin has turned completely white, the person is clean."

God wanted each case of leprosy to be an accurate determination, so the priest had to examine each one and make an exact diagnosis of this debilitating disease. This was very important to God, so the priests were involved because this could affect an entire community. If the skin disease were deep and eating away at the skin, it would lead to that person's exclusion from the entire community. The contamination of that one disorder led to a complete separation from their friends, family, and others. And such an external matter could lead to utter isolation from their world, society, and culture.

White skin indicated that the disease had been healing since it would be "new skin" that had grown over the raw flesh. And in light of this stage, it gave hope for recovery. I love this part of the healing process because it shows us, as God's new creation, that we can overcome our fleshly lifestyle when we give our lives faithfully to Christ and have hope for the future. If someone's leprosy appeared to have gone away, only the priests could decide if that person was cured because they had a duty and responsibility for the well-being and health of the camp.

Throughout scripture, leprosy was viewed as a curse from God and was often connected with sin and those who lived in unsanitary conditions. Although it is generally accepted that leprosy is a chronic disease, which is at some stages infective, such is the fear of the disease that the very name is surrounded with prejudice. This disease remained for years, causing the skin tissues to degenerate and disfigure the body.

Those with leprosy were so despised that they could not live with their family and community of people. As a matter of fact, a leper wasn't allowed to come within six feet of any other human, including their own family. The disease was considered so disgusting that the leper couldn't come within 150 feet of anyone when the wind blew. [1]

The main reason leprosy is talked about so much in the Bible is that it's a graphic illustration of sin's destructive power over a person, community, and culture. In ancient Israel, leprosy was a powerful object lesson of the debilitating influence of sin in a person's life. Lepers lived in a community with other lepers until they got better or died. This was the only way the people knew how to contain the spread of this contagious disease.

Contagious means transmissible by direct or indirect contact with an infected person. When I think of this infectious word, what comes to mind is the effect of today's culture on people's hearts and minds. It is a constant rampage of negative mindsets through social media, the falsehood of conspiracy theories (with no substantiating facts), misleading theology, and the bad attitudes of today's society.

All these evil vices are so negatively shaking that they can become hard to overcome if we allow them to engulf our lives. Why? Because they can lead us to an ill-spirit that becomes contagious and is not Christlike. While leprosy infected the garments and the house's walls, human's sinful ways have infected and scarred all of man's nature. Any type of sin that separates us from a Holy God can be fatal and lead to human destruction—because in it lies spiritual death, if not cured!

Interestingly, it is said that to catch leprosy, a healthy person must have months of close contact with someone with this disease. It's believed that the ill-fated condition spreads when someone with leprosy coughs or sneezes. The infection may spread when a healthy person repeatedly breathes in infected droplets. What is so striking about this analysis is that the longer we're around the activities of sin we will be prone to fall into its deadly spiritual decay.

1. Got Questions, "Why Is Leprosy Talked about?"

Any type of debilitating disease should remind us how our world changed when God pronounced a curse on the earth because of the fall of man. God clearly reminds us in the book of Genesis that His creation was very good and pleasing to Him at one point. However, Adam brought death and decay into the world because he allowed the enemy to deceive them, leading to their disobedience of God's way.

Paul reminds us in Galatians 5:9 that it only takes one wrong person with ways that are not Christlike to infect all the others because a tiny bit of sin infects a great deal of righteousness. Gal 5:7–10, "You were running the race so well. Who has held you back from following the truth? It certainly isn't God, for he is the One who called you to freedom. This false teaching is like a little yeast that spreads through the whole batch of dough! I am trusting the Lord to keep you from believing false teachings. God will judge that person, whoever he is, who has been confusing you."

Jesus also used the word yeast to describe the corrupt teachings of the Sadducees, Pharisees, and Herod in Matt 16:6, 11–12, and Mark 8:15. Like leaven that works its way through the dough, spreading out until its effects are manifest in the entire batch, Jesus warned that the ideas of Herod and the religious leaders were steadily permeating the people's thinking. Even a little yeast raises the whole lump of dough just as "a tiny bit of sin in our life." A small amount of harmful teaching can have a widespread and unholy influence on people's minds and hearts today.

Paul even warned the church at Corinth against tolerating sin that was in their midst, using yeast as a metaphor (1 Cor 5:1–8). There was a man in the church who was guilty of sexual immorality, and Paul told them to remove the man from their fellowship. Because, like yeast, his influence would spread through the whole church. 1 Cor 5:6–7, "Don't you realize that this sin is like a little yeast that spreads through the whole batch of dough? Get rid of the old yeast by removing this wicked person from among you. Then you will be like a fresh batch of dough made without yeast, which is what you really are. Christ, our Passover Lamb, has been sacrificed for us."

Today, there is more focus on all the external infections versus our internal spiritual disease. So many are consumed with everything tearing us apart from the outside, but what about the change in "one person internally?" Including me! Isaiah reminds us that the defilement of our sins separates us from a Holy God, and it's so severe that He's hidden His face from us, and He will not hear us—because a defiled heart is blind and hardened!

As discussed in the last chapter, curing the chronic disease of a defiled heart is allowing the word of God to break our old heart set (Ezek 11:18–21). This will lead to a repentant heart and a humble spirit. It will create a kind, forgiving, and loving person—willing and ready to serve. And that one life of transformation can lead to a societal change that needs to be cured, desperately bad!

Whatever level of contagious sin we have in our lives, we need to discard it and quit allowing it to separate us from the will of God. Instead, we need to rise to a lifestyle of Christlike quality and productivity that's pleasing to our Lord. We must counter the harmful vices consuming us with an active life of genuine worship and fellowship. When we do this, we will see continued thanksgiving, the actual application of God's word in our lives, an ongoing submission to the Holy Spirit, and a fermented daily prayer life.

Prayer changes us by nourishing and strengthening our faith in God. As we communicate with God, we learn He is our Great Provider, and only through Him can we overcome all the contagious obstacles in our lives. Look at the Muslims; they pray five times a day during their entire life, regardless of life's conditions. Jews pray at least three times a day, whether or not they're happy, under attack, or if they've been blessed.

Why do these beliefs take such a strong initiative and stance of prayer so seriously every day? Because that's their lifestyle! They believe it with every fabric of their being! If we want to remove contagious sins in our life, we need to continuously know Who is in control by going to His throne of grace and submitting our lives to Him humbly!

In the New Testament, leaven is also used as a positive metaphor. Jesus said, "The kingdom of Heaven is like leaven" (Matt 13:33; Luke 13:20-21). This passage illustrates an ever-increasing, permeating influence of God's kingdom in the world—and this starts with you and me! If we are going to do anything positive and productive when it comes to being contagious, we need to be "Infectious Builders—Spreading the Kingdom of God!"

> Heb 4:14-16, "So then, since we have a great High Priest who has entered heaven, Jesus the Son of God, let us hold firmly to what we believe. This High Priest of ours understands our weaknesses, for he faced all the same testing we do, yet he did not sin. So let us come boldly to the throne of our gracious God. There we will receive his mercy, and we will find grace to help us when we need it most."

CHAPTER 14

Coming Clean

Lev 14:33–36, 55–57, "Then the LORD said to Moses and Aaron, "When you arrive in Canaan, the land I am giving you as your own possession, I may contaminate some of the houses in your land with mildew. The owner of such a house must then go to the priest and say, 'It appears that my house has some kind of mildew.' Before the priest goes in to inspect the house, he must have the house emptied so nothing inside will be pronounced ceremonially unclean. These are the instructions for dealing with serious skin diseases, including scabby sores; and mildew, whether on clothing or in a house; and a swelling on the skin, a rash, or discolored skin. This procedure will determine whether a person or object is ceremonially clean or unclean. These are the instructions regarding skin diseases and mildew."

THIS MILDEW WAS A dry rot that affected the stone walls. It had to undergo specific cleansing procedures designated for clothes or any building with this withering spoilage. This fungus had to be extinguished and controlled because, if not, it could spread rapidly and promote diseases. In these passages, we see the extreme focus on each detail to ensure it was cleansed so it could not advance.

If there was a severe case of irreparable damage from the fungus, the clothing or the house was destroyed by fire. One keynote is this. God was so detailed in His instructions on removing this mold or fungus and the damage it could create because He cared for the health and protection of His children.

Also, in this passage, we could take away two key points. One, God put the plague there because some of the property in this land was under His judgment due to the people's pagan ways. Or we can look at this passage and see that our Sovereign God causes or allows things to happen for a reason.

So, this leads to a question that many may pose. Does everything happen for a reason? The short answer is "Yes!" Because God is Sovereign, there are no random, out-of-control happenings; God controls everything. All we do in life is either an investment in the flesh or the spirit—and we shall reap in proportion to whatever we have sown (2 Cor 9:6, Gal 6:7–8).

I cannot count the times when an occurrence in my personal life rattled my soul and spirit to its core. I pondered on what, where, when, why, and how. But at a later stage in my life, at just the right time, I realized what happened earlier prepared me for something later.

God is always at work in the lives of His children, and in His goodness, the events that define our lives are not products of natural causes or random chance. They are orchestrated and ordained by God and intended for our good (Rom 8:28). Unfortunately, we often fail to sense God's protection as events unravel or unfold. But in our stages of spiritual growth, when we look back, we can see His working and guiding hand more clearly, even in times of tragedy.

Throughout God's word, He's laid out a personal blueprint to help prepare us for our storms of life, whether trials or tribulations. We must constantly remind ourselves that we will be confronted with temptations, suffering, evil, and the works of the enemy. But God has provided us with the resources to live a godly life that's pleasing to Him, regardless of the things to come. Because through it all, God will be glorified!

There are no promises of a "smooth sailing" life because that does not build our character in becoming more Christlike. When troubles come, we're to consider them an opportunity for joy (James 1:2). We cannot fake our happiness, but we need to learn how to grow in His loving arms of grace, peace, and love while increasing our faith. And our genuine saving faith and His grace will get us through those stages of endurance and perseverance. We will never know the depths of our true Christlike character until we go through intense and severe pressures in this life, including all the blindsides that took us from the peak to the valley!

God intends to ensure that His excellent plan is worked out in our lives, and that's for us to be more like His Son. And to put that power into perspective, look at what Christ went through for you and me. That doesn't compare to what we're going through. God has every intention of you and me becoming more mature, growing in Him, and knowing His purpose and plan will be for our good. Once we grasp that insight, we will not complain about the mold and mildew in our lives, but we will do what we can to remove it by His grace!

Coming clean with the Lord is a critical phase of our daily life. Because, in many cases, when He causes or allows something in our lives, it's to get our attention for a reason (I cannot say this enough). Always remember the beautiful passage in Hebrews chapter twelve, where He tells us we should never ignore it when He disciplines us and not be discouraged when He corrects us. The Lord disciplines those He loves as His children. Our Christian lives involve hard work, requiring all our heart, soul, mind, and strength. And there will be times it will prescribe us to give up whatever endangers our relationship with God.

While God wants us to come clean, the enemy does not want us to confess all our ugliness and weaknesses to the Lord. But once we humble ourselves before His throne of grace, mercy, and love, it can release us from the shackles of burden and weariness. Admitting our wrongs will admonish our pride. And when we "genuinely examine ourselves," it will prove that we're aligned with the Lord's purpose and plan. And that release of heaviness is so fantastic and rejoicing! 2 Cor 13:5–10 and Ps 139:23–24.

> Ps 119:1–8, 165–168, "Joyful are people of integrity, who follow the instructions of the LORD. Joyful are those who obey his laws and search for him with all their hearts. They do not compromise with evil, and they walk only in his paths. You have charged us to keep your commandments carefully. Oh, that my actions would consistently reflect your decrees! Then I will not be ashamed when I compare my life with your commands. As I learn your righteous regulations, I will thank you by living as I should! I will obey your decrees. Please don't give up on me…Those who love your instructions have great peace and do not stumble. I long for your rescue, LORD, so I have obeyed your commands. I have obeyed your laws, for I love them very much. Yes, I obey your commandments and laws because you know everything I do."

CHAPTER 15

God's Temple

Lev 15:1–3, "The LORD spoke to Moses and Aaron: "Speak to the Israelites and tell them: When any man has a discharge from his body, he is unclean. This is uncleanness of his discharge: Whether his body secretes the discharge or retains it, he is unclean. All the days that his body secretes or retains anything because of his discharge, he is unclean.""

Many people avoid this portion of Leviticus because of its graphic depictions. But we need to understand how this applied to the Israelites then and how this applies to us now. When we look at this portion of bodily discharges, it can represent secret sins. God is always concerned about our health, the dignity of our body, and all experiences, especially if they're unhealthy practices.

In this passage, we discover a profound point, in contrast to the previous chapters, regarding the broad definition of leprosy. There is no mention of priestly inspection or monitoring here in this chapter, which means this was done by the individual, which is a pure self-examination!

Almighty God always wants us to promote healthy bodies since they are the temple of the Holy Spirit. Everything we do regarding our bodies must be from the perspective of God's love and control in our lives. He's concerned about our physical and spiritual habits; because they intertwine and represent Him as representatives on this earth! To prevent dirty acts, we must allow God to lead us in all our decision-making, demonstrating that He's "Lord over all our life, and He's part of everything."

How can the Holy Spirit dwell within a proclaimed believer if they continue to allow corruption in their daily life? There is not enough room for the Spirit in our life when there are acts of unholiness. Remember what Paul tells us in Galatians chapter five—there are only two forces at war within us, and they "cannot co-exist." The Holy Spirit counsels and tells us that our bodies are the sacred place—where He wants to live. And if His Spirit is not actively alive in us, how can we worship, admire, and honor Him? God does not convey to us that our body is a home, house, or residence—but it's His holy temple. In other words, our bodies, as believers, were designed to be a shrine or a holy place.

Therefore, how we act, think, and speak, and what we let into the temple through our eyes and ears, becomes critically important. Why? Because every thought, word, and deed is in His view. Nothing is hidden from our Lord, not even one secret sin which could lead to unhealthy practices. Heb 4:12–13, "For the word of God is alive and powerful. It is sharper than the sharpest two-edged sword, cutting between soul and spirit, between joint and marrow. It exposes our innermost thoughts and desires. Nothing in all creation is hidden from God. Everything is naked and exposed before his eyes, and he is the one to whom we are accountable."

As believers and dedicated followers of Jesus Christ, we must realize Who is indwelling within us. It's the same powerful Spirit that raised Christ from the dead. As we've seen throughout this book, anything opposite God's holiness separates us from Him. And when we allow unholy things into our lives, we will grieve the Holy Spirit (Eph 4:30). Paul instructed the Ephesians not to bring sorrow to the Spirit but to "Get rid of all bitterness, rage, anger, harsh words, and slander, as well as all types of evil behavior." Instead, be kind to each other, tenderhearted, and forgiving one another, just as God, through Christ, has forgiven you. (Eph 4:31–32).

Many do not reflect on the importance of treating their bodies with deep respect for God's holiness "that it deserves." Why? Because some people think they can do as they please, while God's word tells us that our bodies are not our own; as Paul said, we have indeed been bought with a price. If a mature and growing Christian grasped the depth of that verse in 1 Cor 6:19–20, they would see this compelling point that sums up how we're to treat our bodies. And that's this. *"So, glorify God in your body."* What does that mean? Our bodies are for the glory of God! We're to use our bodies in ways that will show that God is more satisfying, more precious, more to be desired, and more glorious than anything the body craves.

Paul reminds us "once again" in Galatians chapter five that if we're living by the power of the Holy Spirit, it will produce every element of the Fruit of the Spirit (love through self-control). But if our flesh controls us, it will lead to evil vices that set us apart from God's will. Once again, these two forces cannot co-exist within us; "one controls our life more than the other."

The way we show complete reverence to the body as a temple our Creator has blessed and endowed us with is when our hearts, minds, and spirits have been renewed with thoughts and attitudes that exhibit our lives as His children with acts of righteousness and holiness. And when we instill obedience in our daily life, this blesses our Heavenly Father and shows our ultimate reverence and respect for Him.

> Paul also reminds us in Rom 12:1–2, "And so, dear brothers and sisters, I plead with you to give your bodies to God because of all he has done for you. Let them be a living and holy sacrifice, the kind he will find acceptable. This is truly the way to worship Him. Don't copy the behavior and customs of this world, but let God transform you into a new person by changing the way you think. Then you will learn to know God's will for you, which is good and pleasing and perfect."

God wants us to offer ourselves as a total and complete sacrifice, laying aside any desires our old body craves daily. He wants us to place all our energy (heart, soul, mind, and strength) and resources at His disposal and trust Him throughout our life's journey. In this way, we honor and glorify Him!

CHAPTER 16

Our Approach

Lev 16:1–3, "The LORD spoke to Moses after the death of two of Aaron's sons when they approached the presence of the LORD and died. The LORD said to Moses: "Tell your brother Aaron that he may not come whenever he wants into the holy place behind the veil in front of the mercy seat on the ark or else, he will die because I appear in the cloud above the mercy seat. "Aaron is to enter the most holy place in this way:"

The Day of Atonement was the greatest day of the year for Israel. On this day, Aaron had to spend many hours preparing himself to meet God, and he "could not go" just anytime he wanted. God is giving specific instructions for Aaron (through Moses) on how to make atonement for his house because of the act his two sons committed.

God cares about the ruin of a family through disobedience. That's why He's preserved the sanctity of His Holy Place for those who are pure and cleansed of their transgressions. Even a high priest who was so revered was not exempt. God's requirement for holiness applies to everyone! We must never forget that our God is a Holy God, and we cannot take this privilege of coming to Him for granted and with carelessness because we must be in tune with His divine nature!

Every day, when we approach God, should be special and precious moments as we remember what Jesus Christ did for us on the cross—because His Atonement opened the door for all "who want" to enter! The invitation for believers to come and dwell in His holy presence is available for anyone, no matter who you are. There's no limit or timeframe; it's an open-door policy—it is extended to anyone at any time. But it's how we prepare ourselves before we approach the holy presence of God and His Son.

We need to realize that the magnitude of our approach to a holy God is essential. We can only approach Him in His ways: 1) He expects us to come before Him with complete reverence and respect, 2) He expects an attitude and heart that is Christlike (repentant, forgiving, humble & loving), 3) He expects our desires & motives to align with His purpose and plan for our life, 4) He expects a wholehearted commitment to Him, 5) and He expects absolute faith and trust in all His ways. Eph 3:12," Because of Christ and our faith in him, we can now come boldly and confidently into God's presence. So please don't lose heart because of my trials here. I am suffering for you, so you should feel honored."

The author of Hebrews conveys to us the superiority of Jesus and urges us to follow Him closely. In Hebrews 4:16, the author reminds us: "Let us then approach God's throne of grace with confidence, so that we may receive mercy and find grace to help us in our time of need." So, following Jesus is about confidence and boldness, not timidity. Jesus Christ is our High Priest and intercedes on our behalf today (Rom 8:34). Not only can we come boldly to the throne of grace for forgiveness and salvation, but we also know that we are no longer enemies of God. As firm believers, we are now His beloved children.

It's an unbelievable honor and privilege to approach our Heavenly Father and Creator because of what Jesus Christ did for us on the cross. We have no reason to be apprehensive or discouraged but come confidently and boldly with a heart of humility and respect. Once we accept Christ as the Savior of our lives, we are united with God our Father, and we can go directly to His presence through daily prayer. He now welcomes you and me openly and wants to hear about our issues and concerns of everyday life.

God-fearing children who respect His awe-striking presence are drawn to His holiness and long for His intervention during those tough times. In that complete state of reverence, we come to God because we know He has all the answers in life, and we don't. We need a mindset that always lifts our spirits and hearts toward God with such adoration and distinction—never frowning on the life He has blessed us with so dearly.

We should never approach God because we think our good works are deserving. We should come before Him as an unworthy sinner who has been saved by His amazing grace. And from the depths of our souls and spirit, we're pleading for His mercy while thanking Him for His love and patience. Our approach to God's throne should be with a heart, knowing that our sins must be dealt with daily.

As fallible humans, we're not even capable of removing our sins, and that's when we recognize complete trust and faith in the One who paid the price for us once and for all! And when we're at that point of crying out from the very core of our being, we acknowledge God's provision for removing all our sins through Christ, our Savior, and Redeemer!

We must always approach God with positive persistence, knowing that He will provide for our spiritual good as a Loving Father. And even when we feel that some of our prayers have not been answered, we cannot allow those times in our lives to create a dry spirit and lead us to discouragement or disgruntlement. But draw closer to Him by seeking more of His counsel, guidance, and wisdom. In His timing, He will make it right! Remember this guide—"How we approach God should be the same way we approach others in everyday life."

> Rom 3:21–24, "But now God has shown us a way to be made right with him without keeping the requirements of the law, as was promised in the writings of Moses and the prophets long ago. We are made right with God by placing our faith in Jesus Christ. And this is true for everyone who believes, no matter who we are. For everyone has sinned; we all fall short of God's glorious standard. Yet God, in his grace, freely makes us right in his sight. He did this through Christ Jesus when he freed us from the penalty for our sins."

CHAPTER 17

Our Lifeline

Lev 17:10–11, "Anyone from the house of Israel or from the foreigners who live among them who eats any blood, I will turn against that person who eats blood and cut him off from his people. For the life of a creature is in the blood, and I have appointed it to you to make atonement on the altar for your lives, since it is the lifeblood that makes atonement."

In Leviticus chapter seventeen, God gives instructions regarding sacrifices and offerings, particularly on the proper slaughtering of animals. The people of Israel were to bring each animal to the Tabernacle entrance for the priest to offer. The animal's blood was never to be treated as common food—because it belonged to God, Who is the giver of life (Gen 2:7; Job 33:4; Ps 139:13). Thus, the blood of animals had to be drained and offered to God on the altar because blood was God's ordained means of effecting atonement.

When God says in the passage above, "He will turn against that person," He's simply saying He's rejecting or abandoning them because He knew the practices of the idolater world! In ancient days, when pagan hunters killed any game, they would pour out the animal's blood as an offering to "a" god. Contrarily, the Israelites banned all such actions pertaining to this idolatry, for they knew this was not what God had taught them.

The difference was this. The pagans said: "Life is in the blood; I must eat or drink it and take that life for myself." But the godly said, "The life of the flesh is in the blood, and it belongs to God and not to me." This emphasized a powerful idea and truth—'Life belongs to God' (1 Cor 6:19–20, Col 1:16). Therefore, God sets His face against someone who takes authority over life for themselves.

What a stark contrast in the mindset of one who "does not" understand God's message and does not comply with His guidelines—versus a "godly person who understands His commands and the direction He wants to lead in our lives!" Here's a parable to live by: "From a fleshly perspective, our life depends on blood because it is preserved and nourished by it. And when enough blood leaves a body, life succumbs because blood is the lifeline for our survival."[1] "And from a spiritual perspective, when the indwelling Spirit is not alive in us, we can give way to a life that could lead us down a path of destruction."

Our earthly lifelines are based on our everyday choices and can affect us physically, emotionally, and spiritually. We will either choose a life that is more of the flesh or the Spirit, and it will boil down to this; the desired path that we want to take. This is so important because, too often, we easily get caught up and sucked into a life of self-indulgence, and in those times of selfish desires, we need someone to throw us a spiritual rope so we can stay connected while our rescue is in progress.

If we only knew that our lifeline of support is in our Savior, Jesus Christ, it may change our everyday choices in life—because His help is always available. He constantly reminds us that things will improve if we cling to the right source of life. He can keep us alive and offer that glimmer of light and hope in its darkest times. God's word reminds us in Ps 46:1, "God is our refuge and strength, always ready to help in times of trouble." We must never forget that our lifeline to our Heavenly Father is Jesus Christ, our Savior. But to sustain that lifeline, we need the power of His word and Spirit accessible and at work in our lives to assist us in life-threatening situations. God's word provides all of life's answers from Genesis through Revelation and is breathed by God Himself, which provides the breath of life and is adequate for all good works. And the Holy Spirit leads us through the Bible to all truths.

Is this vital for us to understand in today's time? Unequivocally yes! Because what we're experiencing in life is a culture and society that is steering down the road of no return. What we're seeing more of in life are people taking up habits that they feel are purely innocent and just fun. But habits become very serious when it comes to spiritual matters because they can lead to a habitual pattern of danger. Just ask the Israelites!

As we mentioned earlier in the book, and this is so important, sinful habits can become harmful vices in our daily lives that are heard to break.[2] And when we make these acts a standard way of living, they can become difficult to separate from our daily life. We must never forget that these unhealthy traits can lead to a lifestyle that is not pleasing to our Lord in any way, shape,

1. Enduring Word Ministry, "Sanctity of Blood."
2. Jones, "Our Lifeline Is Christ."

or form. He simply wants His dedicated lifelong children to surrender to His Way, Truth, and Life!

Because when our lives point vertically to Christ, it not only leads us to solid horizontal relationships within our community of believers—but it sustains us temporarily while on this Earth while preparing us for our state of permanency with Him. It establishes our firm foundation of faith in the One that leads us to yield to the power of His Spirit so we can learn to live in obedience and loyalty to the type of life He desires for you and me. When Jesus came and offered His life while pouring out His blood on the cross, the perfect sacrifice had finally been made once and for all. Now His blood pumps everlasting life into us. That precious atonement, which was shed to its last drop of life, is why God takes this so seriously.

Because of what Jesus Christ did for you and me, we're now redeemed, made right with God, and our ransom has been paid. Our sins and guilty consciences are cleansed because He enabled forgiveness. We are now set free, and we've been justified and sanctified. Christ opened the door to God, and we now have a hope, joy, and peace that overcomes the enemy (John 14:27, Phil 4:7). Who in the world would not aspire to this means of escape today?

The one thing we must understand as a student of God's word is this—all sin separates us from God, and because of sin, it costs God dearly, which was the sacrifice and the blood of His only Son. But because of His immeasurable love for His children, we are reunited with the Father—once a believer comes to Christ by faith. His mercy, grace, patience, faithfulness, and love are truly amazing—despite our failings!

All because of a temporary pleasure that humans have desired since the beginning of time and even today led God to establish a place of permanency for those who believe in what Christ, His only Son, did for them on the cross! Our lifeline of eternity rests in a straightforward choice. It's either for a new life in Christ—or to continue the old way of living in the flesh that can never be a part of God's family.

Unfortunately, many still feel like they have the freedom to do what their little hearts desire when "they feel the need to satisfy their flesh." But the author of Hebrews reminds us in Heb 10:26, "Dear friends, if we deliberately continue sinning after we have received the knowledge of the truth, there is no longer any sacrifice that will cover these sins."

As a friend and child of God, staying grounded in the Truth is vital to staying connected with our Lord daily—that is why we must continuously remind ourselves and focus on what Jesus did on that old rugged cross for you and me. Because when we do this, we will consciously aim to live out our liberty in Christ while glorifying God our Father!

For many years, the Navigators have used a helpful diagram of a wheel with four spokes to illustrate the essential elements of the Christian life. 1) one spoke is the word, 2) another is prayer, 3) a third is fellowship, 4) and a fourth is witnessing. But the wheel's hub is Christ, the nucleus that drives an obedient Christian in action. It represents Christ as our lifeline and power supply.

But sometimes we tend to focus so much on the spokes, such as the daily things we should do as Christians, like getting into the word, praying, and serving, that we lose focus on the "main" hub, which is Jesus Christ—the power source for our Christian life. It is not the word of God itself or even prayer that supplies the power and grace to live the Christian life—it is Jesus Christ Who is our lifeline. We must never put so much emphasis on the wheel, which is God's channel of grace, that we lose sight of the hub, Jesus Christ—because He is the source of our life![3]

Hebrews 10:19–25, "And so, dear brothers and sisters, we can boldly enter heaven's Most Holy Place because of the blood of Jesus. By his death, Jesus opened a new and life-giving way through the curtain into the Most Holy Place. And since we have a great High Priest who rules over God's house, let us go right into the presence of God with sincere hearts, fully trusting him. For our guilty consciences have been sprinkled with Christ's blood to make us clean, and our bodies have been washed with pure water. Let us hold tightly without wavering to the hope we affirm, for God can be trusted to keep his promise. Let us think of ways to motivate one another to acts of love and good works. And let us not neglect our meeting together, as some people do, but encourage one another, especially now that the day of his return is drawing near."

3. The Navigators, "Wheel Illustration."

CHAPTER 18

Godless Acts

Lev 18:1–6, "Then the LORD said to Moses, "Give the following instructions to the people of Israel. I am the LORD your God. So please do not act like the people in Egypt, where you used to live, or like the people of Canaan, where I am taking you. It would be best if you did not imitate their way of life. You must obey all my regulations and be careful to obey my decrees, for I am the LORD your God. If you obey my decrees and my regulations, you will find life through them. I am the LORD. "You must never have sexual relations with a close relative, for I am the LORD."

This chapter regarding human sexuality could be the Bible's most extensive and straightforward passage—because it expresses the mind and heart of God regarding sexuality. God explicitly directs this message to His children, the Israelites, for "they were the only kingdom that acknowledged and recognized God as their King." The PowerPoint of this message is where God states," I am the Lord your God." This means they belong to Him and are not to indulge in the ways of the world like in Egypt!

God warned His children to leave every aspect of their pagan background, for they were about to embark on more sinful lifestyles in the land of Canaan. God was helping the Israelites instill and form a new culture of godliness into their everyday lives—because He knew the culture of the Canaanites appealed to worldly desires from a societal and religious perspective. The only way the Israelites could remain pure and be set apart for God's use was to comply and live by the laws He required in their daily life.

He prohibited them from self-absorbing their lives into the surroundings and culture that would lead them away from His purpose and plan. So,

God continuously repeated, "I am the Lord your God," which declares the distinct qualities of the One, True, Living, and Holy God. He called His people to live holy lives because He is holy. This is the one divine essence of God we should chase after in our daily lives.

Sexual immorality is a big deal for many reasons laid out in God's word. Sex was designed to consummate the lifetime union between a man and a woman. Jesus said, "What God has joined together, let no one separate" (Matt 19:6; Mark 10:9). He designed male and female bodies differently so that they could come together in the act of physical intimacy that joins them together for life. They "are no longer two, but one flesh" (Mark 10:8).

The act of becoming one creates a new holy entity: a family, and, within marriage, God blesses it (Gen 1:28; 9:27; Ps 17:3). Sex is a gift to a husband and wife to make their relationship unique among all other relationships. However, what God creates as good, Satan sure knows how to pervert it, so he began his deceitful defilement in the Garden of Eden.[1]

Sexual sin defiles more than just our physical bodies (1 Cor 6:18); it has spiritual significance. Almost every book of the Bible renounces sexual immorality, which is why God considers it a grave sin. Furthermore, committing sexual sin directly opposes God's will to sanctify us (1 Thess 4:3). While the enemy wants to taint our lives with every bit of sin he can, we need to remember this. When Jesus Christ returns, He wants to find you and me as His people who are clean on the inside and outside.

Refusing to acknowledge God's boundaries about this topic opens the door to our fleshly desires. This will only lead to sin and a path far from God's will and plan—because He designed human sexuality between a husband and a wife. When He created man and woman in Genesis, He clearly states, "It was very good!" It also symbolizes our union with Christ and God's unbreakable covenant with His children as His very own.

Unrepentant sexual sin defiles the heart, making it impossible to experience the power of the Holy Spirit in our lives. If we wish to be pure in heart, we cannot engage in sexual sin. As followers of Jesus Christ, we need to peel back the layers of "self" and get to the root cause of sexual immorality. When we yield to the power of God's word and the Holy Spirit's conviction and counsel, we will discover that a central problem of sexual sin is pride.

What springs from the fountain of pride is this: "My desires deserve whatever my heart longs for." The root of pride is the ego, and the ego is based on the flesh. Consider Jesus' words in Mark 7:21–23: "For from within, out of the heart of man, come evil thoughts, sexual immorality, theft, murder, adultery, coveting, wickedness, deceit, sensuality, envy, slander, pride, foolishness."

1. Got Questions, "What Makes Sexual Sin?"

And in Prov 16:18, "Pride goes before destruction, and haughtiness before a fall."

To show us the seriousness of man's ways, God's word reminds us in Rom 1:21–32, "Yes, they knew God, but they wouldn't worship him as God or even give him thanks. And they began to think up foolish ideas of what God was like. As a result, their minds became dark and confused. Claiming to be wise, they instead became utter fools. And instead of worshiping the glorious, ever-living God, they worshiped idols made to look like mere people, birds, animals, and reptiles."

"So, God abandoned them to do whatever shameful things their hearts desired. As a result, they did vile and degrading things with each other's bodies. They traded the truth about God for a lie. So, they worshiped and served the things God created instead of the Creator himself, who is worthy of eternal praise! Amen. That is why God abandoned them to their shameful desires. Even the women turned against the natural way of having sex and instead indulged in sex with each other. And the men, instead of having normal sexual relations with women, burned with lust for each other. Men did shameful things with other men, and as a result of this sin, they suffered within themselves the penalty they deserved. Since they thought it foolish to acknowledge God, he abandoned them to their foolish thinking and let them do things that should never be done."

"Their lives became full of every kind of wickedness, sin, greed, hate, envy, murder, quarreling, deception, malicious behavior, and gossip. They are backstabbers, haters of God, insolent, proud, and boastful. They invent new ways of sinning, and they disobey their parents. They refuse to understand, break their promises, are heartless, and have no mercy. They know God's justice requires that those who do these things deserve to die, yet they do them anyway. Worse yet, they encourage others to do them, too."

The critical component to counter this ugly root of pride and man's ways is Christlike humility. The key to attaining and sustaining this type of humility is cultivating a quality life in the word of God. It requires guidance from the Holy Spirit and prayer for His divine strength. It is taking our eyes off ourselves and surrendering and submitting unto the One Whom all things are possible.

God's word reminds us in Jas 4:4–10, "You adulterers! Don't you realize that friendship with the world makes you an enemy of God? I say it again: If you want to be a friend of the world, you make yourself an enemy of God. Do you think the Scriptures have no meaning? They say that God is passionate and that the spirit he has placed within us should be faithful to him. And he gives grace generously. As the Scriptures say, "God opposes the proud but gives grace to the humble." So, humble yourselves before God. Resist the devil, and he will flee from you. Come close to God, and God will come close to you. Wash your hands, you sinners; purify your hearts, for your loyalty is divided between God and the world. Let there be tears for what you have done. Let there be sorrow and deep grief. Let there be sadness instead of laughter and gloom instead of joy. Humble yourselves before the Lord, and he will lift you up in honor."

The only One we should ever act like or mirror in our daily lives is our Lord and Savior, Jesus Christ! If we obey His words and apply them, our life is one of His peace, patience, contentment, joy, love, and self-control. And this is pleasing to Him, and it nurtures our souls.

CHAPTER 19

Desired Markings

Lev 19:28, "You shall not make any cuttings in your flesh for the dead, nor tattoo any marks on you: I am the LORD."

Depending on the translation, in almost every verse from eleven to thirty-seven in this chapter, you see the declarations, "You shall not," "You shall," or "Do not!" Some may think God's word is a book or letter of don'ts. But this was a profound passage that Jesus told us in the New Testament. "Love the Lord your God with all your heart, soul, mind and strength and your neighbor as yourself," He called these the greatest commandments of all. So, here's the gut punch: When we comply with these two simple great commands with every fiber of our being, we discover that following God's other laws is not difficult!

Marking on the skin or tattoos were pagan practices that God did not want his children to participate in. Why? Because they were all connected with unholy rituals. Examples: The pagans would cut deep gashes in their skin while mourning the death of a relative. This was done to provide life and blood for the dead person's spirit rather than to express sorrow. The tattoo or markings could also indicate that one was a slave to a particular deity and honoring different idols. The bottom line is that these were pagan practices with the wrong motives. We will address more of this later.

So many would say getting a tattoo is an absolute sin because of this verse above. But if that's the case, you must take the entire message of this chapter into context, and here are some examples: In verse sixteen, God's word says, "Don't spread slanderous gossip among your people." And in verse seventeen, God says, "Do not nurse hatred in your heart for any of your relatives, and in verse eighteen, "Do not seek revenge or bear a grudge against a fellow Israelite but love your neighbor as yourself. I am the LORD." And, in verse twenty-six, the Bible tells us, "Do not eat meat that has not been drained of its blood." I would say that almost everyone has violated these laws.

When we start casting stones at others based on one scripture from the Bible, we need to look at God's entire message—because you can almost guarantee there is a verse that applies to you and me. But as we look at the key passage at the beginning of this chapter regarding markings or tattoos, as mature Christians, we must remember the power of perception. Example: Today, how our culture thinks and perceives things is essential, especially when we're to exemplify Christlikeness. If some clothing, jewelry, or other body apparel would associate us with the pagan world, it should not be done.

This is a tricky line to draw because cultural standards constantly go through conversions. But, over time, as a society, we've been able to adjust, adapt and accept various ways of personal change. One small example is today's changing standards of body piercings for men and women. Fifty years ago, who would have thought this would be acceptable to any future generation? Over time, most people have gradually accepted it as the physical norm. However, from a spiritual perspective, as Christians go through their sanctification stages, they start looking at the person's inner heart and their exemplary of Jesus Christ outwardly—versus their skin or physical appearance!

We must look at the Old Testament law that prohibited tattoos before we leave the discussion of skin markings. The reason for the prohibition of tattoos in this passage is not stated. However, tattooing was likely a pagan practice connected with idolatry and superstition. It was probably standard for the pagans to mark their skin with the name of a false god or a symbol honoring some other idol.

God demanded that His children be different, so He reminded them in the same verse, "I am the LORD." The Israelites belonged to Him; they were His workmanship and should not bear the name of a false god on their bodies. While New Testament believers are not under the Mosaic Law, we can take from this command the principle that if a Christian chooses to get a tattoo, it should never be for superstitious reasons or to promote worldly philosophy. The bottom line is that getting a tattoo is not a sin, per se. It is a matter of Christian freedom and should be guided by biblical principles and rooted in love.

Here are some general biblical principles that may apply to getting a tattoo:

- Children must honor and obey their parents (Eph 6:1–2). Violating their parents' wishes is biblically unsupportable for minors to get tattoos. Tattoos born of rebellion are sinful.

- "Outward adornment" is not as important as the development of the "inner self" and should not be the focus of a Christian (1 Pet 3:3–4). A person who desires a tattoo to garner attention or draw admiration has a vain and sinful focus on self.

- God sees the heart, and our motivation for anything we do should be to glorify Him (1 Cor 10:31). Motivations for getting a tattoo, such as "to fit in," "to stand out," etc., all fall short of the glory of God. The tattoo itself may not be a sin, but the motivation to get it might be.

- Our bodies, as well as our souls, have been redeemed and belong to God. The believer's body is the temple of the Holy Spirit (1 Cor 6:19–20). How much modification of that temple is appropriate? Is there a line that should not be crossed? Is there a point at which the proliferation of tattoos on one body ceases to be art and starts becoming sinful mutilation? This should be a matter of individual reflection and honest prayer.

- We are Christ's ambassadors, delivering God's message to the world (2 Cor 5:20). What message does the tattoo send, and will it aid or detract from representing Christ and sharing the gospel?[1]

Maybe the most applicable verse on whether getting a tattoo is a sin would be Rom 14:23, "For whatever does not proceed from faith is sin." If a Christian must ask whether something is right or wrong, it could be a powerful sign that it is wrong. As Christians, we should never do anything unless we are convinced it is right.

Every follower of Christ should act on their convictions from the Holy Spirit. But I will say this: use the M&M perspective, which is the "Message & Motive" behind the tattoo. In your heart, will it be honoring the Lord? Because let's be honest. Some people get tattoos that send the wrong message. As some would say, "Think before you ink."

And whatever, don't be a stumbling block to the weaker in faith (1 Cor 8:9). Our liberty in Christ is not worth another person's walk with God being led astray. We are given great freedoms as Christians, but the greatest is considering others' welfare over our own.

As we grow and become more mature in our Christian life, there will be times when we need to discipline ourselves. This is essential in our maturity stages because we can build up the weaker in faith and not push them into a liberty that they're not ready for. We must never encourage another one to act in a way the Bible identifies explicitly as sin. That is a danger zone! (Matt 18:5–7, 1 Cor 8:9 and Rom 14:13).

---

1. Got Questions, "What Does the Bible Say?"

If there are to be any desired markings in our Christian life that God requires, it is this. It does not consist of rituals, physical markings, and traditions because He wants a heart that is marked with the life of His Son, Jesus Christ. That type of character displays a life that is His and available for use and a purpose to serve Him. If God has our whole heart, the world will see His accurate identification in us.

That is why Paul says, in Rom 12:1–2, "And so, dear brothers and sisters, I plead with you to give your bodies to God because of all he has done for you. Let them be a living and holy sacrifice, the kind he will find acceptable. This is truly the way to worship Him. Don't copy the behavior and customs of this world, but let God transform you into a new person by changing the way you think. Then you will learn to know God's will for you, which is good and pleasing and perfect." When we act upon this fundamental principle, we will yield to Him, act upon our convictions from the Holy Spirit, submit ourselves humbly to Him, and seek His will!

Prov 12:15, "Fools think their way is right, but the wise listen to others."

CHAPTER 20

Be Set Apart

Lev 20:7–8, 22–23 "So set yourselves apart to be holy, for I am the Lord your God. Keep all my decrees by putting them into practice, for I am the Lord who makes you holy." "You must keep all my decrees and regulations by putting them into practice; otherwise, the land to which I am bringing you as your new home will vomit you out. Do not live according to the customs of the people I am driving out before you. It is because they do these shameful things that I detest them."

After God's direction and guidance for each offering concerning His strict laws, rebuking against pagan practices, and instructions for cleansing and godliness, He repeats and reminds His children towards the end of this book a critical point: "Keep all of My decrees and put them into practice, set yourselves apart, and be holy for I am Holy!" After this powerful declaration, the vital and operative statement is: "Put My commands into practice, exercise them, and He can help them to be separate from the world." This is a strong point of application for us today!

Also nestled in this chapter are the penalties for breaking the law, which will lead to punishment for their disobedience. In chapter twenty, God addresses this message to the entire community. He's letting them know their violations against His decrees would receive His justice. He reminds them that they will be dealt with, and He will execute His sentence. Because of the widespread idolatry and pagan practices that consumed the Israelites, they found it difficult to depart from their old lifestyle.

Their old way of life led so many to reject the laws of God, and He could not set them apart for good use. He wanted His children to rest in His principles, provisions, and promises and believe in Him with all their hearts. That is why the author tells us in Hebrews chapter three to be careful and not allow our hearts to harden against the word of God, stubbornly setting ourselves against His purpose and plan. When the Israelites continuously disregarded and disobeyed God's commands, it created a farther distance between them and God.

Hebrews 3:7–19, That is why the Holy Spirit says, "Today when you hear his voice, don't harden your hearts as Israel did when they rebelled when they tested me in the wilderness. There your ancestors tested and tried my patience, even though they saw my miracles for forty years. So, I was angry with them, and I said, 'Their hearts always turn away from me. They refuse to do what I tell them.' So, in my anger, I took an oath: 'They will never enter my place of rest.'" Be careful then, dear brothers and sisters. Make sure that your own hearts are not evil and unbelieving, turning you away from the living God. You must warn each other every day, while it is still "today," so that none of you will be deceived by sin and hardened against God."

"If we are faithful to the end, trusting God just as firmly as when we first believed, we will share in all that belongs to Christ. Remember what it says: "Today, when you hear his voice, don't harden your hearts as Israel did when they rebelled." And who was it who rebelled against God, even though they heard his voice? Wasn't it the people Moses led out of Egypt? And who made God angry for forty years? Wasn't it the people who sinned, whose corpses lay in the wilderness? And to whom was God speaking when he took an oath that they would never enter his rest? Wasn't it the people who disobeyed him? So, we see that because of their unbelief, they were not able to enter his rest."

In the passage above, God's place of rest allows Him to control all things while freeing us from the chaos and disorder brought about by man's sin and rebellion—and this requires our undeniable steadfast faith in Him in every area of our life. We must trust in all His promises daily, hourly, and every beating minute, for without that belief, it could prevent us from entering God's place of rest in Heaven—one that He's prepared for you and me.

God's place of comfort will help and guide us in everyday life—while preparing us for that place of holiness and joy that will satisfy our hearts infinitely. However, if we forsake Him and put our trust in ourselves or in the promises of this world, we could be set apart for something that will not be pleasant. Remember, as God's chosen ones, we were elected to be set apart for a purpose, but we have a responsibility—because that day-by-day, hour-by-hour trust in God's promises is *not* automatic. So, we must make an all-out effort to be set apart for His excellent use.

We can accomplish this through daily diligence in the power of God's word, applying it to our lives, leaning to the Holy Spirit, and believing and obeying all His ways wholeheartedly—for this is the proper fear of Almighty God. We must depart from relying on our own works and way of doing things so we can be set apart for His good plan. When our faith is rested in Christ alone, and we yield to the working of the Holy Spirit, it leads us to complete obedience to Him for all things.

This should be our cry and marching orders every day! "I hear your words Lord, and I want to depart from the ways of the world so I can be set apart for your glory! I want everyone to see Christ in me, but it's hard and seems humanly impossible! But I am going to your word and yielding to the Holy Spirit for guidance because I want more of you and less of me and the world." When we follow these basic orders, we can enhance our Christian life.

Eph 4:13 teaches us this: The more we grow in Christ, the stronger and more unified we will be as a church, for we are His church! The operative word here is more, a greater quantity, an increase, and an addition. 2 Peter chapter 1 is one of the best chapters showing us how to grow in our faith by paying attention to His word.

We will still inhabit a sin-infected body until we are glorified in God's presence in heaven. The struggle against our flesh is constant, even for the most mature Christian (Rom 7:15–24). However, in the Christian life, we should progressively achieve greater and greater victory over sin. But our battle against sin will not end on this side of eternity.

Even the great Apostle Paul reminds us in Phil 3:12–16 that he had not reached perfection but was pressing on toward that heavenly goal (prize). And the secret to that formula is when we read, observe, interpret, apply, grow, and press on in life. And trust me, this is our game changer for the Lord in this world of corruption. We need to depart ourselves from the old ways of life—so we can be set apart in the newness and freshness of Christ.

Prov 3:1–7, "My child, never forget the things I have taught you. Store my commands in your heart. If you do this, you will live many years, and your life will be satisfying. Never let loyalty and kindness leave you! Tie them around your neck as a reminder. Write them deep within your heart. Then you will find favor with both God and people, and you will earn a good reputation. Trust in the LORD with all your heart; do not depend on your own understanding. Seek His will in all you do, and He will show you which path to take. Don't be impressed with your own wisdom. Instead, fear the LORD and turn away from evil."

CHAPTER 21

Our High Calling

Lev 21:16–17, "Then the LORD said to Moses, "Give the following instructions to Aaron: In all future generations, none of your descendants who has any defect will qualify to offer food to his God."

Chapter twenty-one lays out specific guidelines for the priests because they had a high calling from God. He chose them for a purpose, and that was to serve God with their lives by offering sacrifices. The priests of God not only had a high calling for service unto God, but if they did not comply with all of His guidelines, it could cost them their lives.

Their calling from God was serious and could be dangerous if that representative did not follow all His rules and regulations. Example: The two sons of Aaron—Nadab, and Abihu, were struck dead for exercising their priestly duties in a way that dishonored God. When a man makes any effort from their fleshly perspective to achieve anything in the eyes of God, failure is inevitable. It can only be accomplished by the guidance and obedience of God's word through the power of His Spirit (1 Sam 2:22–24).

But in this passage above, God set a stringent guideline for all the priests. It's not that He was discriminating against handicapped people when He said, "None of your descendants who have any defect will qualify to offer food to his God." The critical point here is this. When God told the priests that they could only offer an unblemished animal as the sacrifice for the sins of that person, the same applied to the priests. God is stating that any of them with a spiritual handicap could not offer a sacrifice that would be acceptable and pleasing to Him. Why? There could be no inkling of unholiness in the presence of a Holy God!

This is not an insult. But this is an example of perfection as closely related to God's holiness, which He required and expected. Therefore, any spiritual deformation cannot be in anyone representing our Holy Lord! Of course, we all know that we will never reach the perfection of Jesus Christ (our perfect Sacrifice and High Priest), but this is even more reason to follow God's word and all His ways. This is why we must work toward Christlikeness and lean to the power of the Holy Spirit for help. Only when we put forth an all-out effort to live in all His ways can we offer a body of service and sacrifice pleasing to God!

God's word reminds us in 1 Pet 2:9–10 that as His chosen people, we are a kingdom of priests, His very own possession. As believers in Jesus Christ, He chose you and me to be a part of His holy and royal Priesthood so we can show others the goodness of God. Our genuine saving faith and relationship with Jesus Christ takes our eyes and focus off us; it leads us to represent Him fully, with no intentional shortfalls.

Because as His representatives and ambassadors on this earth, we must remember that our actual value comes from being His chosen ones, serving Him with every fiber of our created being. It should always be considered the highest of privileges that we must always take with exceeding honor. It's not what we achieve in our efforts but showing the worth of what we can do—because of Him working in and through us. The Lord Jesus Christ has instituted a new priestly order, not of a few select individuals but of all who are born again and united by faith with Him.

As Christians, we are now part of God's Priesthood—entrusted holy members of the family of God. As we have seen above, God takes the sin of His priests and representatives seriously because being near God brings a high standard of conduct. As His Priests on this earth, we must never allow the encouragement and compassions of this world to affect us spiritually. If we do, it clouds our regard for the holiness of God. We must know our boundaries of truth and falsehood in this culture of unholiness. If not, it could dull our discerning sense of judgment, and we could lose a total grasp of the significance of what we are doing for our Lord. It is our God-given function and charge to serve God first, then others with Christlike JOY (Jesus, Others, You).

Let's face it and be honest. The most troublesome part of being a Christian is trying to be one of God's representatives in a culture that does not want Jesus. It is no small task, and we cannot do it on our own. We need to be living students of His word with the guidance of His Spirit. Just like the Priests in the Old Testament, God has given us rules for how to serve and interact with others.

And just like then, they are challenging to follow today. But if everyone claiming to be a genuine Christian followed those rules to the T, our world would be a very different place. If His word and Spirit are alive and at work in us, we will act in ways that align with His values and not the world. Always remember—God's ways are always better than our own. He reminds us in Isa 55:8–9, His ways and thoughts are above ours. And when we follow all His practices, our lives, and world will improve (little by little). In many ways, by leaps and bounds of faith when we are in His place of rest.

God is calling all His chosen ones upward, by the voice of the Lord Jesus. He desires us to be Partakers of our holy and high calling. But in this heavenly call, we must always lean upon Him and yield to the power of His Spirit. The words from our Lord Jesus Christ are to be taken with the deepest of regards and respect. He calls us in the person and voice of Christ, "Come unto me," which means we must always be in the attitude mode of Christlikeness, striving for new heights of glory!

Phil 2:3–5, "Don't be selfish; don't try to impress others. Be humble, thinking of others as better than yourselves. Don't look out only for your own interests, but take an interest in others, too. You must have the same attitude that Christ Jesus had."

CHAPTER 22

Practicing Progression

> Lev 22:31–33, "You must faithfully keep all my commands by putting them into practice, for I am the LORD. Do not bring shame on my holy name, for I will display my holiness among the people of Israel. I am the LORD who makes you holy. It was I who rescued you from the land of Egypt, that I might be your God. I am the LORD."

God gave Israel four reasons why they should keep His commandments; 1) Who He is (Their Lord & God), 2) What He is (Holy), 3) What He's doing (making them holy), and 4) what He's done (rescued them from bondage so He can be their God!). Faith in His word illustrates that they would be walking in His righteousness, exemplifying His love for others and, most importantly, glorifying God in the process.

God re-emphasized and reminded them of Who He was and how they could honor Him by putting His commands into daily practice. If not, it could lead to them disgracing God's Holy name and dishonoring Him through disobedience. For years the Israelites had a pattern of leaning toward ways that were not honoring God. But regardless, His love, faithfulness, and promises to His children would stand true through the test of time. Even though they got complacent and out of God's plan, His words of power and action would bring them back to the life that points to Him!

To receive God's complete guidance, we must seek His will in all we do. Solomon tells us in Proverbs chapter three that we're never to forget what we've been taught! We're instructed to store His commands in our hearts and never let that loyalty and kindness elude us. If we ingrain them in our minds and hearts and live by them, we will find favor with God and people. We will attain a good reputation, not because of what we've done, but what He's done in our lives.

The only way we will ever achieve and attain the progression of Christ-likeness is when we concede to our own understanding and chase after the wisdom and knowledge of God's word. Clinging to all His faithful teachings and living by them is our sign of progression. We will not find peace, joy, and comfort if we neglect or ignore any part of His scripture, which teaches and counsels us in all His ways (2 Tim 3:16–17).

Instead, we will experience grief and sorrow. And not only are we self-imposing misery in our lives when we don't lean on Him, but we're grieving the Holy Spirit—it's a rippling effect of spiritual regression! That's why practicing biblical and spiritual progression in our Christian lives is so important.

Progression is developing or moving gradually toward a more advanced state. It's "the normal progression from junior to senior status." A spiritual perspective is from "immature to mature." When we progress in our spiritual walk, it's due to a continuation of our faith in Christ and allowing the power of the Holy Spirit to move us forward and enable Him to work out Christlikeness. When we yield to Him, we will conform to His ways, transform into a new life, and perform acts that glorify Him, no matter the barriers we face.

It's a full-time career of putting into action an absolute resolve of succession by attaining and sustaining the holiness of God in our life. How can we achieve this? By staying connected with every sequence of God's commands. Make no mistake; God is not concerned about our perfection because He knows achieving this in our sinful nature is impossible. But He cares very deeply about our spiritual progression toward His holy standards. Why? Because it demonstrates our faith and obedience to His word and reflects our sanctification progress in this Christian life. While we can never fully know God and all His ways, we can all seek Him and walk in a manner where we observe, interpret, and apply the richness and fullness of His word and grow in His wisdom. And this is the path to Christlikeness!

Sometimes when we get stuck, we want to give up because we're in that old rut again! A life that points to "us alone" will lead to discouragement and loneliness. So, here are four practices of progression we can add to our lives: 1) make Christlike changes in your life, 2) take steps of holiness, 3) defocus from your old life & refocus on your new life in Christ, and 4) renew your mind and heart. Four simple sayings—but it's easier said than done for many.

As a Christian, it's simple. We're either progressing "or" regressing in our Christian walk (ouch)! To get away from a complacent life or out of that rut, we must be content and grow in what the Lord has instilled in us! 2 Pet 1:8–9 reminds us, "For if these qualities are yours and are increasing, they do not make you useless nor unproductive in the true knowledge of our Lord Jesus Christ, for the one who lacks these qualities is blind or short-sighted, having forgotten his purification from his former sins."

If we're not progressing, it's not because of God—it's because of the shortfalls we're allowing in our lives. These defects or inadequacies are the active sins leading us to lose and not gain ground, which can be major setbacks. That's why our efforts of Christlike progression reflect the genuine attitude of our hearts.

We must leave our old selves behind "once and for all" and experience our new life in Christ. This is vital, not only in our own lives but for the sake of others. When we're living our new Christian life, others will see a progressed believer that points to Jesus Christ through you and me! What an excellent and powerful way to plant and water seeds.

Col 3:10–11, "Put on your new nature, and be renewed as you learn to know your Creator and become like him. In this new life, it doesn't matter if you are a Jew or a Gentile, circumcised or uncircumcised, barbaric, uncivilized, slave, or free. Christ is all that matters, and he lives in all of us."

CHAPTER 23

Grateful or Ungrateful

Lev 23:1–3, "The LORD said to Moses, "Give the following instructions to the people of Israel. These are the LORD's appointed festivals, which you are to proclaim as official days for holy assembly. "You have six days each week for your ordinary work, but the seventh day is a Sabbath day of complete rest, an official day for holy assembly. It is the LORD's Sabbath day, and it must be observed wherever you live."

God established festivals and days throughout the seasons (every year) for times of rest, fellowship, worship, and remembering with thanksgiving all the things God had done for them. These special feasts were given only to the children of Israel with a rich symbolic significance that they belonged to God. He gave them to His children with the primary purpose of gratitude, praise, and honor to God for all He had done and how He continues to provide. These events displayed God's undeniable mercy and lovingkindness, which applies to us today. Each of these feasts played a purpose in their lives during each season. Here's a list of the appointed festivals below.

1. Passover reminds us of redemption from sin.

2. The Feast of Unleavened Bread is a remembrance of their haste in preparing for their Exodus from Egypt.

3. The Feast of First Fruits occurred at the beginning of the harvest and signified Israel's gratitude to and their dependence upon God.

4. The Feast of Weeks (Pentecost) occurred 50 days after the First Fruits and celebrated the end of the grain harvest, showing gratitude to God.

5. The Feast of Trumpets commemorated the end of the agricultural and festival year. The trumpet blast was meant to signal that Israel was entering a sacred season.

6. The Day of Atonement was the day the high priest went into the Holy of Holies each year to make an offering for the sins of Israel.

7. The Feast of Tabernacles (Booths) is the final feast of the Lord. For seven days, the Israelites presented offerings to the Lord, during which time they lived in huts recalling their prior residence before taking the land of Canaan (Lev 23:43)

God appointed these days to be kept in honor of His name. These times of celebration are essential not only to Israel but also to the overall message of the Bible. Because each one foreshadows or symbolizes an aspect of the life, death, and resurrection of the Lord Jesus Christ!

The festivals hold timeless significance for Christians because they show God's plan of salvation for humanity. That's why we must reflect and recollect everything God has done for us through His Son, Jesus Christ. We symbolize our thankfulness and appreciation to God when we live a Christlike life daily while displaying a deep heart of sincere gratitude.

If we lose the spiritual sense of showing genuine gratitude to God for all He's done for us, we can lose focus on the central point of who Jesus Christ is in our lives. And when that presence is absent, we no longer focus on His blessings and take them for granted. Perhaps the most famous instance of ingratitude in history is in the New Testament gospel of Luke.

Jesus heals ten lepers of their physical disease and, in so doing, of their social disgrace. Once pronounced clean of their contagious condition and no longer social outcasts, they would get their old lives back. How would they respond or react? You would think they would be overwhelmingly grateful after they were renewed and refreshed, right? However, only one returned to express thanksgiving (gratefulness) for being healed. See Jesus' comments in this powerful passage below!

Luke 17:11–19, "As Jesus continued on toward Jerusalem, he reached the border between Galilee and Samaria. As he entered a village there, ten men with leprosy stood at a distance, crying out, "Jesus, Master, have mercy on us!" He looked at them and said, "Go show yourselves to the priests." And as they went, they were cleansed of their leprosy. One of them, when he saw that he was healed, came back to Jesus, shouting, "Praise God!" He fell to the ground at Jesus' feet, thanking him for what he had done. This man was a Samaritan. Jesus asked, "Didn't I heal ten men? Where are the other nine? Has no one returned to give glory to God except this foreigner?" And Jesus said to the man, "Stand up and go. Your faith has healed you."

Jesus healed all ten lepers, but only one returned to thank the Lord for what He had done. A key takeaway is this; only the man with a thankful heart learned that his faith played a genuine role in his healing. And here's the gut punch. Only grateful Christians grow in a clear understanding of God's grace!

So, this makes me wonder. Why were the nine other lepers, healed by God's mercy and love, not as grateful as the one who was? The nasty nature of ingratitude has existed for thousands of years, and we see swarms of this selfish behavior in our own society today. Why?

Contemporary research paints a more complicated picture of ingratitude. Ungrateful people tend to be characterized by excessive self-importance, arrogance, vanity, and an unquenchable need for admiration and approval. Unappreciative people could also be called narcissists because they expect special favors and feel no need to pay back or pay forward any favor at all.[1]

This is becoming more widespread today than ever because people seem to succumb to more self-indulgence—and God's word confirms this in Ecclesiastes chapter two, Matt 23:25, 1 Tim 5:6, and 2 Tim 3;2–9. God does not desire this hideous trait, so we must ensure we do not fall into the wrong group.

Make no mistake about this, in life, there are going to be two groups of people that will surface:

1. The grateful believer who acknowledges an Ever-Loving God with perpetual thankfulness, cheerfulness, and joyfulness for God's provision because they recognize and acknowledge His goodness and loving-kindness. Regardless of the circumstance or outcome, they know "It's His will be done, not theirs." They constantly display the Fruit of the Spirit—not saying they are perfect, but they strive for more "godliness versus godlessness."

2. Or the ungrateful heart, who has "no sense" of feeling, loving, belief, faith, patience, accountability, repentance, and obedient heart. They are selfish, possess unstable emotions, are consumed with secularism, and feel like the world owes them everything. They have no foundation for Christlikeness!

We need to know which group we fall into because out of these two will rise two classes of people, either the "encourager or discourager." The encourager is looking for the best results, not just for themselves but for the sake of others. They have the disposition of gratefulness because they see life through a set of spiritual lenses that say, "There are brighter days ahead because God is

---

1. Emmons, "What Gets in the Way?"

always good." It's in their nature to encourage others around them—because they see the big picture of God's blessings in their lives.

But in comparison, a discourager is all about themselves, with no accountability. They focus on what they don't have and live a life of gloom and doom. And in many cases, they want to bring everyone down to their level. Think about this power statement: "It's easy to deflate a person—but uplifting others takes a heart of great insight and intentional willingness." Look at some of the qualities of an encourager below, but also the deficiencies or inferiorities of a discourager.

- The Christian encourager, who has leaned upon the grace of God through the most challenging times, yields these types of by-products in their daily life. 1) they are optimistic builders for Christ; 2) they exemplify patience, peace, contentment, and joy; 3) they help the weaker in faith and are not stumbling blocks; 4) they stray away from revenge because they are a peacemaker; 5) they continuously pray with thankfulness and praise; 6) they don't make it a chore to stifle the Holy Spirit; 6) they avoid all evil acts; 7) they count on God's constant help and counsel through the power of His word and Spirit; 8), they dwell in the land of forgiveness and love; 9) they continuously edify and encourage the body of Christ, and 10) they work toward all acts of fruitfulness. These attributes come from a genuinely grateful person who knows how to lift others up around them! The second epistle of Timothy is a beautiful guide in how the faithful Christian can be an encouragement to others.

- Contrarily, the discourager is a depriver of confidence and lacks self-esteem. They're insecure and possess no hope or spirit of a good outcome. They're disheartening and are spiritually afflicting and annoying. They can beat you down with words and deeds that are depressing and distressing because they are intimidators and false imitators of Christ. They exhibit discontentment and a life of toxic irritability. They are troublesome and put up many spiritual barriers in those around them. These corrupt vices are rooted in an ungrateful person!

It is a proven fact that a genuinely grateful person encourages to build up the body of Christ and not break it down—because they aim to inspire, promote, or advance the church—they will do all they can to support the entire body. At the same time, the discourager will be opposing and difficult attempting to obstruct God's plan—because their target is to hinder the work of Almighty God. They will cause the body of Christ to become depressed and dejected, while encouragers will help people find confidence and boldness. They are all about digression, not progression!

Today, more than ever, the body of Christ needs more active encouragers—because the devil prompts the discouragers from accomplishing God's plan. In Nehemiah chapter four, we see a great example of how low-spirited enemies can ridicule the believer, leading to discouragement and despair. While the opponent tried to dissuade God's children from achieving His plan of rebuilding Jerusalem's walls, the faithful continued for the Lord's cause and moved forward with faith. In these times of woes, we need to go to God for encouragement and strength and never forget His promise that He's with us! Ps 46:1 reminds us, "God is our refuge and strength, always ready to help in times of trouble."

This is important for believers because a grateful heart always possesses a positive outlook for the future—they aspire to encourage the benefit of God's purpose and plan. On the other hand, an ungrateful person inherits an opposing view and wants to break down the entire system! No matter the seasons of life, we cannot allow the latter to permeate because they can steal your joy. Their primary goal is to rob your spiritual bank of thankfulness and deprive you of praise.

Being a grateful Christian is an important attribute—because it can open the eyes, minds, hearts, and spirits so that others can see God's goodness in His children's lives. It's the avenue that can plant and water seeds of His Righteousness in the unbeliever's heart. It will show the world that God is closer to His beloved ones than the unrighteous may think. When our soul and spirit send the emotional signals of God's presence in our daily life, it could be the only opportunity for that "one" person to see the reality of God's Supremacy and Goodness in the life of a grateful Christian.

However, many could say, "Giving thanks for my current condition is difficult." But here's the PowerPoint. Giving thanks is the one thing we must do to see God's will accomplish in our lives, like the one leper who was a Samaritan. Paul tells us in 1 Thess 5:16–18, "Always be joyful. Never stop praying. Be thankful in all circumstances, for this is God's will for you who belong to Christ Jesus." He doesn't say often, sometimes, part of the time, or whenever you feel like it. He says we should always be joyful!

We're going to endure various conditions and occurrences in our lives that will, at times, seem brutal. But no matter what, our joy, prayers, and thankfulness to the God of mercy, grace, and love cannot fluctuate. In other words, don't waffle, waver, or cave in, but stand firm in the faith of God's will. When we lean toward the power of faithfulness during burdensome times, we will find it much easier to endure and persevere.

The key to having a grateful heart is coming clean before God's throne of grace. What does that mean? If there are any impurities in your life, they must be dealt with first! 1) Confess and repent for all sins, 2) pray with a heart of godly motives, aligning ourselves with God's purpose and plan, 3) yield to the Holy Spirit when He aims to convict, counsel, and comfort, 4) comply to all of God's word and 5) possess a heart of thankfulness, generosity, and contentment.

Let's face it, we all go through our seasons of life. Some good, some bad, and some ugly. We're reminded in Eccl 3:1 that "There is a time for everything, a season for every activity under Heaven." There's a plan for each of us, and there will be cycles in this journey of life. Every experience we go through has a rich spiritual significance for that appointed time because it's God's will.

The secret to having God's peace through these seasons is to accept & believe in His plan. God has given us something special, and His Spirit's power reminds us we can "depend on Him" throughout these trying periods (Ps 46:1). But the great news is this. He reminds us that there's a special day set aside for His children. A day with a lasting solution that points to a lifelong season of peace and rests for all who have accepted and believe in their Savior, Jesus Christ! When our minds and hearts are in this disposition of life, it will be easy to live as a grateful child of God while encouraging others to do the same.

> Eph 5:15–20, "So be careful how you live. Don't live like fools, but like those who are wise. Make the most of every opportunity in these evil days. Don't act thoughtlessly but understand what the Lord wants you to do. Don't be drunk with wine because that will ruin your life. Instead, be filled with the Holy Spirit, singing Psalms and hymns and spiritual songs among yourselves, and making music to the Lord in your hearts. And give thanks for everything to God the Father in the name of our Lord Jesus Christ."

Our daily measuring stick should be based on this: Are we like the one "grateful" leper who *recognized* that he was healed by a Loving and Merciful God—or the nine "ungrateful" lepers who did not acknowledge the Master Healer?

CHAPTER 24

Destructive Words

Lev 24:10–16, "One day, a man who had an Israelite mother and an Egyptian father came out of his tent and got into a fight with one of the Israelite men. During the fight, this son of an Israelite woman blasphemed the Name of the LORD with a curse. So, the man was brought to Moses for judgment. His mother was She-lomith, the daughter of Dibri of the tribe of Dan. They kept the man in custody until the LORD's will in the matter should become clear to them. Then the LORD said to Moses, "Take the blasphemer outside the camp, and tell all those who heard the curse to lay their hands on his head. Then let the entire community stone him to death. Say to the people of Israel: Those who curse their God will be punished for their sin. Anyone who blasphemes the Name of the LORD must be stoned to death by the whole community of Israel. Any native-born Israelite or foreigner among you who blas-phemes the Name of the LORD must be put to death.""

Almost one-third of this chapter focuses on just punishment for anyone curs-ing God. It may have been common for the foreigners to curse their many gods, but not the Great I Am, the Lord Most High! But if we pay close atten-tion to this opening passage, we may discover what instigated God's name to be blasphemed by the son of an Israelite woman. It's one of the root causes that applies to us today, and it was this—"when they got into a fight." In other words, the flesh got the best of him!

But another critical point is this: Did you notice that this son who blasphemed God came from a mother who was from God's chosen people (Israel) and an apparent pagan father, who was an Egyptian? This is a classic example of the importance of raising a child in a godly environment that must be rooted with a spiritual leader (father) and a god-fearing woman—who are both on God's page of divine guidance and values.

It was a principle of justice for anyone who blasphemed God to be put to death. Its first emphasis is upon this: Those who plan to enter the Kingdom of God, and enjoy its privileges, must be governed by God's laws of purity and holiness, not of this world. This means anyone intending to enter His Heavenly Realms is to renounce all other lordships that reign in their life. Godly citizens are expected to accept God's statutes and ways and live by them. And "there's no exception to His rules."

Blasphemy is whenever anything is used regarding God's Holy name that signifies the speaking of Him in an ungodly nature of His attributes or works. It's a contempt toward God with a defiance of irreverence. In English, "blasphemy" denotes any utterance that insults God or Christ in any shape or form. Why would any proclaimed Christian spew words or acts that downgrade His holy name? Because He's to be consistently praised for all things, exalted to the highest— not lowered or defamed!

This punishment for blasphemy (cursing God) would seem extreme by modern standards. Still, God's justness and fairness should show us how seriously He expects us to take our relationship with Him—because it's either genuine and always loving or insensitive and cold-hearted.

A true believer in the God Most High will never utter any derogatory or inflammatory choice of words in any setting against Him, His Son, and the Holy Spirit! To blaspheme the Holy Spirit is different because it is not an act of ignorance; it is an act of willful defiance. Blasphemy against the Holy Spirit is the unpardonable sin, the state of continued unbelief!

And this leads me to a valid point that many overlook—the Holy Spirit does not get His due in our lives. After all, He's the Spirit of God, the Spirit of the Son, the One that dwells within us as believers—and is the same power that raised Christ from the dead. This is the same powerful Spirit that enables us with gifts to perform our Lord's tasks as His Citizens of Heaven on this earth.

He is equal in nature and is attributed to the Father and Son. Christ said He is the One who "will lead us into all truths." Without His guidance, we cannot get one step ahead in our Christian walk. He convicts us when we're out of line, counsels us to get us back in line, and comforts us when we don't feel like we're in line. When you see a Christian with humility and the exaltation of Christ is one that enjoys the Holy Spirit's privileges at work.

Gal 2:20–21, "My old self has been crucified with Christ. It is no longer I who live, but Christ lives in me. So, I live in this earthly body by trusting in the Son of God, who loved me and gave himself for me. I do not treat the grace of God as meaningless. For if keeping the law could make us right with God, then there was no need for Christ to die."

When we're truly living as God's children of the Light and maturing in our daily walk, we recognize our words are either; 1) loving or hateful, 2) graceful or rigid, 3) joyous or miserable, 4) uplifting or tearing down, 5) praising or condemning, 6) honoring or dishonoring, 7) worshipping or despising, 8) good or bad, 9) kind or cruel, 10) positive or negative, 11) full of empathy or apathy, 12) controlling or untamed, and there's no in-between.

Followers of Jesus Christ are held to a higher standard than the unbelieving world, and that's why we're responsible for ensuring that our behavior doesn't incite others to curse God. We should not be minimizing the power of God but maximizing our efforts in proclaiming Who He is. In Rom 2:17–24, Paul scolds those who claim to be saved through the law yet still live in sin.

This leads to another concern: those who use ungodly words of shame and disgust "more" than godly words of praise, love, and grace. So, is cursing a sin? Let me bring this to your attention: People who practice cursing are controlled "more" by the flesh than the Holy Spirit (Galatians chapter five)! God's word reminds us in Ephesians chapters four and five and in Colossians chapters three and four that we cannot imitate a Holy God when we allow foolish or crude talk, foul language, or any corrupt talk to come from our mouths. As Christ-followers, the words from our lips should be those of love, honor, thanksgiving, and grace.

James even reminds us in the third chapter of his epistle that the same mouth that flows out blessings also spews out cursing, which is dishonorable to God. This is critical for God's children to understand because it can destroy our witness for Jesus Christ! When we live a life of instability, and we're imbalanced because of our flesh, it can lead to us being more of a stumbling block than one building on the foundation of Jesus Christ. This type of behavior is a defeater in our Christlike walk, not a victor.

Cursing is not valuable in helping others—because a mouth of the flesh and world does not lift you or anyone else up spiritually. And probably just as important, when we habitually use foul or ungodly words, it creates a gateway for more sins, such as those in Galatians chapter five. It can open the floodgate to many destructive acts, such as using God or Jesus Christ's name in vain.

Getting rid of unpleasant words from our mouths is like giving up a bad habit. We cannot accomplish this in our own strength, but the Holy Spirit can help us learn to incorporate more self-control in our choice of words, especially in those heated moments. One key focal point is this. It is spiritually vital that we do not surround ourselves with the corrupt words spewed through social media, people, and a world of hate. But meditate and memorize the richness and fullness of God's Word that is layered with love, grace, joy, peace, patience, self-control, and forgiveness (Col 3:16 and Ps 1:2 and Ps 119:1–8). We can all surely live by Solomon's words in Prov 16:24, "Pleasant words are like a honeycomb, Sweetness to the soul and health to the bones,"

We must never forget the power of Jesus' words in Matt 15:18 when He taught the Pharisees about inner purity. He says, "The words we speak come from the heart, which defiles us." So many of us work hard to look our best from the outside, but God is more concerned about what lies in our hearts. If we apply His word to our lives, yield to the Holy Spirit, and pray for strength in our weakest areas, He will continue to change and enable us to have healthy thoughts, actions, and those words that are pleasing to Him. So many try but fail in this attempt to get rid of foul language. But never give up because God is worthy of all our efforts!

Those who want to tame their tongue possess a repentant heart with a divine intention to control their fleshly reactions; it contains a spiritual maturity that responds with a willingness to the Lord of complete surrender and submission with humility and love. He will forgive the sin of blasphemy and even that ugly mouth. Example: Paul was a blasphemer (1 Tim 1:13) and tried to make others blaspheme (Acts 26:11). Jesus' own brothers and family thought He was insane and wanted to seize Him (Mark 3:21). But all repented, and all were forgiven.

Blasphemy, by definition, is both deliberate and direct and so often layered with such vile language. That being the case, a believer in Jesus Christ will not and cannot commit blasphemy—because a genuine follower of Christ will try to eliminate the choice of bad words coming from their mouth. With this in mind, we should reflect God's holiness and never misrepresent His glory, authority, and character in all areas of our daily life (Col 3:17).

2 Tim 2:15–21, "Work hard so you can present yourself to God and receive his approval. Be a good worker, one who does not need to be ashamed and who correctly explains the word of truth. Avoid worthless, foolish talk that only leads to more godless behavior. This kind of talk spreads like cancer, as in the case of Hymenaeus and Philetus. They have left the path of truth, claiming that the resurrection of the dead has already occurred; in this way, they have turned some people away from the faith. But God's truth stands firm like a foundation stone with this inscription: "The LORD knows those who are his," and "All who belong to the LORD must turn away from evil." In a wealthy home, some utensils are made of gold and silver, and some are made of wood and clay. The expensive utensils are used for special occasions, and the cheap ones are for everyday use. If you keep yourself pure, you will be a special utensil for honorable use. Your life will be clean, and you will be ready for the Master to use you for every good work."

CHAPTER 25

Breaking Oppression

Lev 25:9–19, "Then on the Day of Atonement in the fiftieth year, blow the ram's horn loud and long throughout the land. Set this year apart as holy, a time to proclaim freedom throughout the land for all who live there. It will be a jubilee year for you when each of you may return to the land that belonged to your ancestors and return to your own clan. This fiftieth year will be a jubilee for you. During that year, you must not plant your fields or store away any of the crops that grow on their own, and don't gather the grapes from your unpruned vines. It will be a jubilee year for you, and you must keep it holy. But you may eat whatever the land produces on its own."

"In the Year of Jubilee, each of you may return to the land that belonged to your ancestors. When you make an agreement with your neighbor to buy or sell property, you must not take advantage of each other. When you buy land from your neighbor, the price you pay must be based on the number of years since the last jubilee. The seller must set the price by taking into account the number of years remaining until the next Year of Jubilee. The more years until the next jubilee, the higher the price; the fewer years, the lower the price. After all, the person selling the land is actually selling you a certain number of harvests. Show your fear of God by not taking advantage of each other. I am the LORD your God. "If you want to live securely in the land, follow my decrees and obey my regulations. Then the land will yield large crops, and you will eat your fill and live securely in it."

The Year of Jubilee was designed to be celebrated every fifty years, which included canceling debts, freeing all slaves, and returning to their original owners all that had been sold. This event would restore the families and free the land from the bondage of debt, as all mortgages would be canceled. The purpose of this year was to break the oppression of the people and end financial hardship—so slaves were set free, and mortgages ended.

Every fifty years, the Israelites would have a year of rest. But one keynote in this chapter is this; slavery was a slightly different custom in ancient Israelite times than in our modern-day views. Israelites would keep captives of war, which would fall into a separate category of slavery. But the slavery referred to in this passage was a slave who owed his master money. During the year of Jubilee, bondservants would be freed from their debts and could return to their own homes as free men.

However, there are no records in God's word that this event was ever implemented, but there are instances like in Nehemiah chapters eight and ten. Still, it was not faithfully administered as God recommended. This makes me wonder; if they had followed this plan set forth by God, they would have lived in a nation or society without poverty. Because if we look at the power of God's message to them in verses 18–19, we see they had the choice to obey this regulation and be fruitful but apparently failed to do so. "If you want to live securely in the land, follow my decrees, and obey my regulations, then the land will yield large crops, and you will eat your fill and live securely in it." God's children were called and challenged to trust Him and acknowledge in a life-changing way that He would be their provider of the necessities of life.

God promised that if Israel obeyed Him, He would provide them with so much in the sixth year that they would not only be supplied for the seventh year when they gave the land rest, but they would also be eating the produce some three years later after the sixth year— (wow, what an abundance of blessings). The promise was so sure that God said He would command it! Today, if we obey God, no matter what, we can trust He will provide our every need. If we seek first the kingdom of God and His righteousness, all those practical things will be provided (Matt 6:33).[1]

Why was this event, the "Year of Jubilee," so important to God? It's simply this; our Heavenly Father loves rest because it enables His children a time to renew, refresh, and reinvigorate their lives for a purpose and plan that will glorify Him through obedience, love, service, worship, thanksgiving, praise, and genuine fellowship.

And today, our ultimate rest is found in Jesus Christ. He invites all who are "weary and heavy burdened" to come to Him, cast all our cares upon Him—and He will give us rest from the worries of the world (Matt 11:28; 1 Pet 5:7). This is so important because His place of comfort relieves us from this

1. Enduring Word Ministry, "Special Sabbaths and Jubilee."

life's sorrows, pains, and sufferings. Our Lord and Savior can free us from all these burdens if we willingly surrender them to Him. The rest Jesus promises is one with love, spiritual healing, and peace with the Heavenly Father. And that type of firm and solid relationship with Christ can transform life's meaningless and wearisome labors into effective spiritual changes.

But also, a significant reason this event was so important to God is because He hates bondage. It's evident throughout scripture that God does not approve of anything that holds His children in fleshly oppression—for that's not the liberty of service He desires in our lives. If we're to be servants, it's under the authority of God through His Son, Jesus Christ, with administered power through the Holy Spirit.

The Jubilee portrays a beautiful picture of the New Testament themes of redemption and forgiveness. Jesus Christ is our Redeemer Who came to set free those who are slaves and prisoners of sin (Rom 8:2; Gal 5:1; 3:22). The debt of sin we owe to God was paid on the cross as Jesus died on our behalf, and we are forgiven the debt forever (Col 2:13–14). We are no longer in bondage and slaves to sin because Christ freed us. We can now enter the rest that God provides as we cease our "own" laboring so we can make ourselves acceptable to our Heavenly Father (Heb 4:9–10).

Many Israelites experienced deep-rooted oppression during these times, as if they were emotionally and spiritually strapped down. A sense of oppression can be associated with feeling trapped, restricted, insecure, lacking confidence, uncomfortable, hesitant, controlled, disrespected, and helpless. And make no mistake; this is one area where the enemy can attack us because Christians sometimes feel oppressed by the ways of their surrounding society, culture, friends, family, and community.

In addition, we can feel tormented by constant cravings—those little desires that we know are not of God. Then we deal with those compounding factors such as lack of approval, physical ailments, or emotional problems such as moodiness, anxiety, fear, worry, and depression. These can be so spiritually debilitating that they will bog us down into the ruts of deepest despair and make us feel like we're in bondage daily!

And unfortunately, we have those times of self-imposed oppression when our inner criticism kicks into high gear—where we beat ourselves to the point of hopelessness. This meltdown occurs when our pride supersedes, and we all tend to over-emphasize a matter in our life because we're trying to resolve it on our own. In other words, we have not given it entirely to the Lord. What I mean by over-emphasizing is *that we treat something more important than is needed*, which can lead to oppression because our flesh is looking for the answers. Good luck! If we would spend all that time over-emphasizing a matter in the word of God and submit to His grace and power, His truth will come to the surface and be of more assistance in our time of need!

Breaking oppression, when feeling subjected to hardship, misery, cruelty, persecution, or any level of abuse, lies in this—seeking the truthfulness of God's word. Because in it lies the essential attributes of His love, guidance, and the strength and security to free us from any bondage that prevents us from a life of liberty in Jesus Christ. We must remember that the work of oppression is a state of falsehood and false identity of who we truly are as God's children. We cannot allow the enemy to blind us in this mindset but believe in what God's word tells us.

So, when our Lord says, "I tell you the truth," which accurately represents fact, why don't we have enough faith to believe this? God wants to deliver and convert us from the ways of the world that can hold us in bondage with "stinking thinking" that produces failure in so many ways (Rom 12:1–2). God desires to give us freedom by applying His truths of faith and love. He has revealed Himself as the Way, the Truth, and the Life. Do we believe it? Will we discipline ourselves to use the Truth to its fullest?

God's word reminds us powerfully in these passages, 1 John 4:6, "But we belong to God, and those who know God listen to us. If they do not belong to God, they do not listen to us. That is how we know if someone has the Spirit of truth or the Spirit of deception." Paul even reminds us in Gal 4:16, "Have I now become your enemy because I am telling you the truth?" John 8:32, 45 conclusively tells us, "And you will know the truth, and the truth will set you free." So, when I tell the truth, you just naturally don't believe me!"

Since the truth about God is vitally important, the New Testament emphasizes the need for "sound doctrine" (1 Tim 1:10; 2 Tim 4:3; Titus 1:9; 2:1). We need to be grounded in the truths of God's word and believe it and live it out because it can make the difference between life and death (John 5:24; 8:24; 20:31). When we observe, access, and apply the absolute truth and knowledge of God's word into our daily lives, and allow His Spirit to lead us, we will be able to acquire a highly developed sense of the root cause of our oppressed life (2 Cor 13:5, Jas 1:23–25, Lam 3:40). Then, with God's help, we will realize our inseparable goodness, integrity, and strength and allow Him to rescue us from self-imposed oppression.

Ps 9:9–10, "The LORD is a shelter for the oppressed, a refuge in times of trouble. Those who know your name trust in you, for you, O LORD, do not abandon those who search for you."

CHAPTER 26

Blessings or Curses

Lev 26:2–4, 14–17, "You must keep my Sabbath days of rest and show reverence for my sanctuary. I am the LORD. "If you follow my decrees and are careful to obey my commands, I will send you the seasonal rains. The land will then yield its crops, and the trees of the field will produce their fruit.... "However, if you do not listen to me or obey all these commands, and if you break my covenant by rejecting my decrees, treating my regulations with contempt, and refusing to obey my commands, I will punish you. I will bring sudden terrors upon you, wasting diseases and burning fevers that will cause your eyes to fail and your life to ebb away. You will plant your crops in vain because your enemies will eat them. I will turn against you, and you will be defeated by your enemies. Those who hate you will rule over you, and you will run even when no one is chasing you!"

This is a remarkable chapter where God promised blessings to an obedient nation—or curses to a disobedient Israel. His children had the great opportunity to benefit from Almighty God if they complied with His commands—or suffer if not. To receive something from God, we must: 1) Be spiritually positioned to hear from Him through His Word and Spirit. In other words, have an open heart, mind, and spirit; 2) Possess a loving, forgiving, repentant, and humble heart; 3) Come to Him with confidence and faithfulness, be open and honest; 4) Be willing and accepting to His purpose and plan, and 5) Trust Him through it all!

Before the blessings and curses are proclaimed, God reminded Israel of this statement: "*The God of Israel alone must be worshipped*," the type of worship that Paul describes in Rom 12:1–2, "And so, dear brothers and sisters, I plead with you to give your bodies to God because of all he has done for you. Let them be a living and holy sacrifice, the kind he will find acceptable. This is truly the way to worship Him. Don't copy the behavior and customs of this world, but let God transform you into a new person by changing the way you think. Then you will learn to know God's will for you, which is good, pleasing, and perfect."

God had to set forth these choices before His children because the Israelites were continuously warned over the worship of their false idols, which were inadequate, insufficient, and worthless; they could never bring value to the throne of God. So many of us today may ask, "After all they had experienced from a Holy God, how could the Israelites deceive themselves with objects of wood, stone, and other materials?" But then I look at some idols we've placed in our own lives today, ahead of the Lord!

We must remember as we look in the mirror and honestly examine ourselves that any type of idolatry or the worship of false idols is hazardous—because it creates a space where we choose possessions, desires, and works of the flesh and the world over God. While the word of God warns us of these idols (like He did to the Israelites), many of us aren't even aware that we're worshipping them. This is a danger zone!

In many translations of Leviticus chapter 26, God says "I will" over 20 times, but He also says "if" at least nine times. God will act and react to His children in how they respond to the "ifs"! He would either bless them so much that the world would know only God could have done this —or curse them so much that not only did God allow this, but He still enabled them to survive. Regardless, the choice was to follow His commands of obedience, which would yield blessings, or disobey Him, which would lead to curses. It would all hinge on the depth of their walk and closeness with God.

When walking with God, He can show us ways of restoration, maturity, and increased faith that are pleasing to Him! Only then, during these progressive stages in our life, can we get clear directions on the commands that He's set before you and me. If Almighty God plainly predicts pain or punishment for "passing pleasures"—or blessings that will yield its good for His glory, who would not want to choose the latter? Sadly, the one with a pattern of living in a world of passing pleasures is dominated by the flesh, not the power of God's Spirit! It's all about their self-desires, not God's desires, which can lead down a destructive path because they're blinded from the True Light!

So, how can we make significant efforts to attain complete obedience? I'm not saying we will reach perfection, but the key is "Continual Fellowship" with the Lord. According to 1 John 1:1–8, genuine fellowship is a daily relationship with God. And this type of fellowship occurs when God's peace and presence continually dwell within us. It happens when Jesus takes up residence in our hearts and minds, and we're allowing His word and Spirit to lead and guide us every day of our life. This kind of companionship acknowledges His power and glory in everything we do—because it leads to authentic worship, which is the highest form of praise, demonstrating complete obedience to Him and His Word. To do this, we must know God personally and intimately, always in sync.

God's word reminds us in Amos 3:3, "Can two people walk together without agreeing on the direction"? This is a beautiful portrait of man's response to God because of his practical obedience, his communion of heart, and his will that aligns with God's plan—this is described as "walking with" or "before God." Incorporating this fellowship with Jesus Christ in our lives will produce a relationship that will lead to significant spiritual blessings and impact you and others in these ways below.

- Establishes a solid companionship and oneness with a faithful and loving confidante, knowing He's always there and you can trust Him for all things, John 15:15, Heb 3:6, Ps 34:18.

- Elevates our prayer life, quality time in His word; applying it to our lives, and yielding to His Spirit, Mark 11:24, Phil 4:6, 1 Thess 5:16–18.

- Personalizes our genuine worship and praise, 2 Cor 1:3–4, Job 1:20–21, John 4:23–24

- Creates a life of Fruitfulness (love, joy, peace, patience, goodness, gentleness, kindness, faithfulness, and self-control) Gal 5:22–23.

- Leads to complete submission to His power and will. Jas 4:7

- Forms a life of forgiveness and contentment in Him, Col 3:13, Matt 6:25–26.

- Shepherds an obedient life demonstrating Christlikeness. Rom 8:29

This pattern of life will lead to Faith working through Love, for it avails anything, Galatians 5:6. Always remember this vital passage in Heb 11:6: "And it is impossible to please God without faith. Anyone who wants to come to Him must believe that God exists and rewards those who sincerely seek Him."

Faith in Jesus Christ is the devoted attachment to Him as Lord and Savior. It's the power of our motivated Christian life, which is the mainspring of our actions that are always in motion. Jesus reminds us in John 14:14, "If you love Me, obey My commandments." Genuine saving faith causes a real follower to seek and do the will of their Lord, while true love tells them what that will is and to obey it.

This powerful claim amplifies this personal saying from Jesus Christ—that the desire of the believer who loves His Lord so deeply will possess genuine Christlike obedience. This type of real love will produce supernatural obedience supplied with pure and righteous motives, leading to a willingness to follow all the Lord's ways. It can only be accomplished if we're in the Light, where we will be spiritually blessed and experience unbelievable fellowship with our Lord and others. However, if we're dwelling in the darkness of this world, we will be so far apart from God's will that we can never experience the blessings and fellowship that He has in store for you and me.

Eph 1:3–8, "All praise to God, the Father of our Lord Jesus Christ, who has blessed us with every spiritual blessing in the heavenly realms because we are united with Christ. Even before he made the world, God loved us and chose us in Christ to be holy and without fault in his eyes. God decided in advance to adopt us into his own family by bringing us to Himself through Jesus Christ. This is what he wanted to do, and it gave him great pleasure. So, we praise God for the glorious grace he has poured out on us who belong to his dear Son. He is so rich in kindness and grace that he purchased our freedom with the blood of his Son and forgave our sins. He has showered his kindness on us, along with all wisdom and understanding."

CHAPTER 27

Vows of Value

Lev 27:1–2, 9, 11–12, "The LORD said to Moses, "Give the following instructions to the people of Israel. If anyone makes a special vow to dedicate someone to the LORD by paying the value of that person, here is the scale of values to be used . . . "If your vow involves giving an animal that is acceptable as an offering to the LORD, any gift to the LORD will be considered holy . . . If your vow involves an unclean animal, one that is not acceptable as an offering to the LORD, then you must bring the animal to the priest. He will assess its value, and his assessment will be final, whether high or low."

In this last chapter of Leviticus, we see God teaching the Israelites the importance of when they make a vow to Him. They must keep their promises, even if it costs them more than expected. The Israelites were required to give or dedicate certain things to the Lord; the first fruits of their harvest, firstborn animals, firstborn son, or a tithe of their increase. Many Israelites would go beyond God's recommendations by dedicating themselves, another family member, additional animals, their home, or even a field to God!

But sometimes, they would make rash decisions or unrealistic vows to the Lord. And if they did, there could be a 20% penalty enforced upon their decision if they decided to purchase something back. It was not a sin to refrain from making a vow (Deut 23:22), but once it was made, it had to be kept (Deut 23:21–23; Num 30:2; Eccl 5:4–6).

Psalm 15:4 describes a righteous person as one "Who keeps an oath even when it hurts and does not change their mind." And Jesus' teaching in Matthew chapter five also supports this biblical principle. A vow is binding, even when spoken frivolously or privately. A promise is a promise, and there is no loophole in God's eyes that would allow a person to renege on such a commitment. Our words are powerful, and how we use them as a means of obligation to others will reflect our genuine relationship with our Heavenly Creator.

Our words are the primary source of how we communicate and connect with people. That is why we must speak the truth, live up to our words as accountable Christians, and refuse to speak slander or words that can break our connection with God as Christian representatives.

Committing wholeheartedly to doing something as believers can set the bar for our Christlike integrity, trustworthiness, dependability, and accountability. And this is vital in our Christian life. Why? Because a hasty decision that prevents us from keeping our word could be a detriment and, most importantly, damage our testimony as representatives of Christ.

And if not thought through with spiritual clarity, it could create more problems in our life, especially if we have not taken it to the Lord first (Prov 16:3, Ps 37:5). Because, so often, a quick & hasty vow is made from acts of foolishness, immaturity, or impatience. God's word reminds us in Col 3:17, "Whatever you do or say, do it as representative of Jesus Christ, giving thanks through Him to God the Father."

In the book of Judges (11:29–40), we see the story of Jephthah, a Judge, a man controlled by the Spirit and even listed in the Hall of Faith. He was noted for being a mighty man of courage but made a rash and foolish vow that was costly and would lead to severe consequences. Before leading the Israelites into battle against the Ammonites, Jephthah made an impulsive vow to the Lord. He told God, "If you give me victory, I will give to the Lord the first thing coming out of my house to greet me when I return in triumph. I will sacrifice it as a burnt offering."

When the Lord granted him victory, his daughter was the one who came out to meet him first. Jephthah then remembered his vow and offered her to the Lord. This one example shows us the repercussions of a foolish or premature vow, which can bring unspeakable grief if we do not take it to the Lord so that we can ascertain His guidance.

God calls us to keep our word, so we should do whatever we can to set up guardrails to help us fulfill that call. But we must be sure that we don't get caught up in the heat of the moment emotionally and make promises in the future that are humanly impossible to keep. This is vital because God desires obedience in our daily lives. If we have that close-knit relationship with Him—we will be more prone to take it up with Him first before making a foolish decision.

We must always remember that our words of commitment are crucial, and we can never underestimate their importance. God wants our words to represent Christlikeness in building others up, edifying, encouraging, and not breaking down or discouraging others. And to show us the importance of our words, Jesus reminds us in Matt 12:36–37 that our words are so critical that we will give an account of what we say when we stand before the Lord Jesus Christ. Jesus said, "But I tell you that men will have to give account on the day of judgment for every careless word they have spoken. For by your words, you will be acquitted, and by your words, you will be condemned."

Devoted Christ-followers are those whose hearts have been changed by God's power, a change reflected in their words and genuine commitment. Think about this, "Our words can be full of blessings to others when our hearts are full of God's obedience!" So, if we fill our hearts with the love of Christ, only the truth and purity can come out of our mouths. If anything, let the power of our words be motivated by the Holy Spirit so they manifest the power of our faith in the Lord. When we're faithfully committed to Jesus Christ for the words we convey from our mouths, we will allow Him to be the bridle of every bit coming from our lips!

The only way to prevent from making hasty vows is by attaining more of God's wisdom. Because it is the power to see and the readiness to choose the best path with the surest means of achieving it. Wisdom is, in fact, the practical side of moral goodness and is only found in its fullness in God. To tap into God's divine understanding, we must first desire and ask Him for it. God's word reminds us in Jas 1:5, "If any of you lacks wisdom, you should ask God, who gives generously to all without finding fault, and it will be given to you." But the key is in the next verse, which specifies that we must "ask in faith, not wavering."

To have knowledge is to have understanding or information about something. But to have wisdom is to possess the ability to apply knowledge to everyday life's choices. In reading and understanding God's Word, we obtain knowledge, which brings forth wisdom. But we must be doers of the word, putting it into daily practice.

The book of Proverbs is full of God's wisdom, which calls for hearing and actual doing. To have the "fear of the LORD" is to have an awe of who God is and a reverential trust in His Word and His character, and to live accordingly, which will prompt us to make better choices in life.

When one is walking in fear of the Lord, they rely on God's wisdom in everyday life and will make whatever changes need to be made that God's Word commands—it will be demonstrated in their lives. James reminds us in his epistle (3:13), "Who is wise and understanding among you? Let them show it by their good life, by deeds done in the humility that comes from wisdom." [1]

Also, in James's third and fourth chapters lies a beautiful roadmap for learning to control our tongues and attain genuine wisdom that will lead to a closeness with God. When we incorporate these steps below in our daily life and lean on His power and guidance, it illustrates the worth of God's working wisdom in our lives. If our faithful hearts are aligned with Him, He will lift us up despite our ignorant shortcomings. The key is:

- Humbling ourselves before God.

- Resisting the devil, and don't allow the enemy to entice us.

- Purifying our hearts and being cleansed from sin.

- Let there be sorrow and deep grief for our sins.

- Bowing before the Lord, and He will lift us up.

- Seeking His true wisdom and applying it in our daily life.

- And drawing close to God, and He will draw close to you and me.

The only way we can draw near to a Holy God—so He will draw to us is by ensuring our motives and desires align with His ways of holiness. Coming to Him with a humble heart, mind, and spirit will demonstrate that our absolute commitment is a true sacrifice and promise to God. Not only are our words an offering unto the Lord, but also our possessions, finances, representative as a spouse, believer, workmanship, our service, prayer life, fellowship, and worship. These are all examples of godly sacrifices unto our Lord.

Real sacrifices offered to our Heavenly Father draw you and me closer to Him because it will demonstrate if our intentions truly desire to be near Him. If we want to sustain our value of closeness with Him, our offerings to Him must be accurate and display our commitment with value and genuineness. "Draw near to God, and He will draw near to you."

Prov 18:1–7, "Unfriendly people care only about themselves; they lash out at common sense. Fools are not interested in understanding; they only want to air their opinions. Doing wrong leads to disgrace, and scandalous behavior brings contempt. Wise words are like deep waters, wisdom flows from the wise like a bubbling brook. It is not right to acquit the guilty or deny justice to the innocent. Fools' words get them into constant quarrels; they are asking for a beating. The mouths of fools are their ruin; they trap themselves with their lips."

---

1. Got Questions, "How Can I Tap?"

Summary

Discern Holiness!

In this marvelous book of Leviticus, we have seen many guidelines God set before His people at the foot of Mt. Sinai. And from His commands, we can learn so much about His divine character and the one true essence He requires from His children then and today, and that's holiness. Once we peel back all the layers and dig into the depths of God's instructions in this book, we can hear Him speaking and revealing that He's the same yesterday, today, and tomorrow! His guiding principles have been set forth and laid out, and He reassures us they're suitable for all times. While the world and culture are changing, God's ways at work in us should never change, waver, and be compromised! And that should be our genuine commitment to the Lord as His children in these final days.

As we've seen in this journey throughout Leviticus, and even in our society today, acts of unholiness are surfacing each passing day increasingly, and they're impossible to avoid. God's plan for the Israelites was to prepare them to let go of their sinful ways and pursue His holiness—so they could be set apart for the will of serving Him. It was important then and even so today because God is trying to develop and equip us all for the temporal days now and the eternity that awaits! And the one essential component we need to get us over all the hurdles in life is God's wisdom!

That's why "discernment" is probably one of the most important spiritual gifts bestowed upon us as Christians because it's a step towards the wisdom of God that can perfect our faith. It can enable us with the potential to decide between truth and falsehood, right and wrong, good vs. evil, and wisdom from foolishness. Discernment is accurately evaluating ourselves, people, and situations. God's word reminds us in 1 Thess 5:21–22, "But test everything that is said. Hold on to what is good. Stay away from every kind of evil."

When we study the word of God, over time, we gain knowledge, but that knowledge only leads to wisdom when spiritual discernment is present.

Obtaining this precious gift sets us on track for more of God's wisdom, where we come to value and treasure properly and effectively those things that we believe are pure and righteous. And this type of wisdom demonstrates everything about our faith. It reveals who the Lord of our lives is, God or the world! Therefore, now more than ever, every believer must pray for a discerning spirit, a zeal for holiness, combat apostasy, and contend earnestly for the faith. We must ask God for more spiritual wisdom to aid us in our walk of faith and mature us in the Fruit of the Spirit and our loyalty to His word.

God's word reminds us in James 1:5–8, "If you need wisdom, ask our generous God, and he will give it to you. He will not rebuke you for asking. But when you ask him, be sure that your faith is in God alone. Do not waver, for a person divided loyalty is as unsettled as a wave of the sea that is blown and tossed by the wind. Such people should not expect to receive anything from the Lord. Their loyalty is divided between God and the world, and they are unstable in everything they do."

We are all called to seek and utilize discernment. Prov 17:24 tells us, "Sensible people keep their eyes glued on wisdom, but a fool's eyes wander to the ends of the earth." We are to set our eyes on wisdom because thousands of things on this Earth are competing for our attention and trying to control us daily. Because our hearts are deceitful, we cannot stake our life decisions upon our feelings (Jer 17:9). That's why we must seek the wisdom of God—obtain and sustain it every day of our life on this side of Heaven!

Spiritual discernment is gaining spiritual guidance and understanding by setting our eyes, minds, heart, and souls on the wisdom of God, which starts with the fear of the Lord. When we have the proper fear of the Lord, it illustrates our great awe (Ps 33:8), bestowing honor, deep respect, and gratitude (1 Tim 1:17), and trembling before God (Phil 2:12). This means that we understand our insignificance and magnify the greatness of who God is. The scripture also states that to understand, we need to know the Holy One, and the only way to achieve this is by knowing God intimately. This powerful gift is more necessary now than ever to protect us against false teaching, dabbling in the ways of the world, and walking a path of unholiness.

The enemy aims to obscure our vision with the wrong motives and desires. This often leads to an uncontrollable, topsy-turvy, disordered, and deranged life—going every way it pleases—opposite God's ways. But when we make God's divine nature our top priority in life, that is when we see structure, discipline, accountability, and a legitimate course in life that is pleasing to Him. We must remember this key takeaway; these last days are consumed with ways contrary to God's righteousness and holiness. So, as faithful followers of Jesus Christ, we need a clear path of godliness.

We must adequately self-examine our daily Christian life (2 Cor 13:5, Ps 139:23–24). "If there is no other name but Jesus Christ as Lord of our lives, then there should be no room for anything else that separates us from His will." When something unrighteous creeps into our life, the gauge of our spiritual barometer should fire off that will prevent the flesh from deviating our lives from the holiness of God. We should know by now to flee—because our fight for holiness is a daily struggle!

Although today's society is suppressing the Truth and running after the ways of this world, our ongoing marathon after God's holiness is vital in drawing us closer to Him—because it is the binding tie of unity that enables God's presence and availability in our lives! The world will place every potential obstacle before us to keep us far away from God—so we must press forward because God desires holy living (1 Pet 1:14–16).

Why does God desire us to live a life of holiness? Because the only way we can be valuable and productive for our Lord is to be set apart or separate from the ways of the world. God is holy, and we cannot attain holiness when corruption is present!

God's word tells us in Rom 12:21, "Don't let evil conquer you, but conquer evil by doing good." God's way constantly challenges our fleshly nature and calls us to live at a higher standard by the Spirit's power at work in us. We must always focus on the Lord and His ways because lawlessness will break us down and separate us from a loving and Almighty God—Who has a purpose and plan for our good. You and I are called to a higher standard of discernment. Our choice in pursuing God's most divine nature of holiness "Can Make a Difference in our life, and it will affect others around us!"

In Closing

Embrace Holiness

Too often, Christians don't want to embrace holiness because they consider it an impossible standard. They run away from it because it makes them feel uneasy, seems too pious, alienates people, and makes them feel awkward; it takes them out of their fleshly comfort zone. Some may naturally sense that God's most essential nature has dangerous overtones because His purity calls our sinful parts of life into question. He demands that we desert them so we can enjoy His goodness and righteousness. In our quest, God is not leading you and me to an unattainable level of perfection. However, our shortcomings of godly perfection should spiritually motivate us to make great efforts to obtain God's greatest attribute in our daily lives, all for His glory!

Once again, I am not saying that we can reach perfection, but we must aim for something as Paul did in Phil 3:12–16, "I don't mean to say that I have already achieved these things or that I have already reached perfection. But I press on to possess that perfection for which Christ Jesus first possessed me. No, dear brothers and sisters, I have not achieved it, but I focus on this one thing: Forgetting the past and looking forward to what lies ahead, I press on to reach the end of the race and receive the heavenly prize for which God, through Christ Jesus, is calling us. Let all who are spiritually mature agree on these things. If you disagree on some point, I believe God will make it plain to you. But we must hold on to the progress we have already made." Paul embraced the life of following His Savior; he did not let the past overshadow His life that God set before him.

Here is the mindset that we should have as Christ-followers: "Count yourselves dead to sin but alive to God in Christ Jesus" (Rom 6:11). Any time we face temptation, we should say, "I'm dead to that because it was part of my old life, and I am a new creation in Christ!" (2 Cor 5:17). To live a life pleasing to our Lord, where we separate ourselves from sin, we must see ourselves as God does—born-again children of the Most-High, clothed with the righteousness of Christ, and striving for more of Him in our daily lives.

The holiness of God is a critical facet of His character because He desires, even commands, that His people accept this primary attribute enthusiastically. Emulating a lifestyle that reflects God's character is so essential that the writer of Hebrews urged Christians to "Work at living in peace with everyone, and work at living a holy life, for those who are not holy will not see the Lord." (Heb 12:14). The statement in this passage, "Without holiness, no one will see the Lord" depicts a sense of the author's anticipation of seeing Christ at His excellent return (see 1 John 3:2). This is the culminating point of the broader passage captured in (Heb 12:22–29). If our goal is to be more like Jesus Christ and see Him when He returns, our daily pursuit of Him is vitally important. Paul reminds us in Ephesians 5:5 that no immoral, impure, greedy, or worldly person will inherit the Kingdom of God.

Our growth and sanctification stage started when we were given a new life through the power of the Spirit because of our faith in Jesus Christ. This is critical because, without this, our pursuit of God is in vain. The result of our ongoing Christlike progression is an illustration of Jesus' death and resurrection, which should reflect His ongoing work of holiness in our lives (Col 1:22; 1 Thess 5:23; 2 Thess 2:13; John 3:5–8; 1 Cor 6:11).

We should be motivated by the knowledge of this truth because it will demonstrate whether we're all-out for Christ. If so, the world will see our new nature and the embodiment of moral and righteous ways (Eph 4:24). As believers in Jesus Christ, acts of purity should be alive in our daily life (no ifs, ands, or buts). But we also must remember this crucial step, if our lives are not fitted with the "total" armor of God (Ephesians chapter six), the solidity of our fight in this battle we're experiencing could be futile, and our survival rate could be dim.

We cannot miscalculate this severe point. We're in a battle for the holiness of God because our Christian faith is and will always be in a ceaseless onslaught against an ever-evolving society of lawlessness, which is swaying away from all acts of spirituality. It's advancing in a manner that our God-given spirit anguishes over daily because it is moving expeditiously in a never-ending pattern, one evil drift after another. It's striking us from every area of our Christian walk. And if we're not careful, it can affect our hearts, mind, and attitudes in so many ways (that are not Christlike); we could succumb to this undercurrent, which could affect us and others.

Even when we embrace holiness and pursue it with all we have, there will be times when we will get blindsided. And even in these stages of our life, will Christians still sin? Yes! But do they willfully continue in sin? No! Scripture indicates that while we will always "fall short of the glory of God" (Rom 3:23), we have the hope that the power of God is at work in us to "make us more and more like Him as we are changed into his glorious image" (2 Cor 3:18). And that's the ultimate life-changer that will secure and reassure us in these final days that Christ is truly the Lord of our lives and not this world! As Christ-followers, the key to our growth, maturity, and sanctification in our stretch to become more Christlike is to know that we're sustaining the test of these times (2 Cor 13:5, Col 3:1–10, Romans chapter eight, 1 John 1:8, Ps 139:23–24).

Paul tells us in Philippians chapter two that God works in us to will and act according to His purpose and plan. When we enable His Spirit to produce fruitful works in our daily life, it proves that we're effectively employing the work of our salvation. Once we are justified before God through Christ, it is followed by sanctification, becoming pure, righteous, and holy for His good works—and our fruit-bearing lives follow this. Then, we move forward in our spiritual growth and maturity, being set apart for God's use by His grace.

Our sanctifying stages will include breaking away from the love and power of sinful ways. And instead, we will pursue obedience and steadily and gradually renew our lives to become more Christlike through the power of the Holy Spirit. Working out our salvation demonstrates Who is truly Lord of our lives as devoted servants. As a result, the world sees a royal priesthood of specific people who don't need to be called anything but holy children—growing in godly ways and allowing the Holy Spirit to continue to shape them in the likeness of Jesus Christ.

So, I beg the question. How serious is the one essential nature of God's holiness in our daily life? Do we truly understand the value and importance of living this type of life? To be in the presence of a Pure and Sovereign God, we must veer away from all impurities in life that keep us from His presence because a Holy God cannot be a part of anything impure.

Remember, our evil vices separate us from His holy ground. But regardless of the declining effects of godliness, God expects you and me to respond as His righteous ones, as Isaiah did in chapter six of his book—and not react to an ungodly society with acts of the flesh. We must realize that we need a Holy God in today's times of unrighteousness. We must humbly submit our wholehearted commitment to His ways so that we can be set apart for His use with all the love, mercy, and grace He abounds.

However, the odds in this depraved world are stacked heavily against us because a powerful current is sweeping across the face of this earth. It's a draft of blatant wickedness and impure acts of unrighteousness. The acceptance and practice of evilness are all around us, and there's no escaping. So, I don't know who is in a better place, the salmon swimming upstream to their spawning grounds or us Christians trying to live pure and blameless lives in a depraved world.

Christians, if we would only take a step back, reflect on where we came from since the creation of time, and observe where we're going, God's true children would get a glimpse of the widening gap between holiness vs. unholiness. The distance from one side to the other is growing farther and farther apart. We must seriously ponder our lives from a temporal perspective and then to our permanency state. Look at our family, friends, neighbors, and surrounding community; when unrighteousness is rampant, we must intervene with Christlikeness by God's grace and love. We cannot get complacent in our own little world and forget that we're in an upstream current against the ways of our Holy God.

Unless there is a change that includes a person embracing and harnessing God's holiness in their daily life, it is to be feared that what we'll see is a falling away from the genuine Christian faith. The apostle John signifies this is a mark of a false believer: "They went out from us, but they were not really of us; for if they had been of us, they would have remained with us; but they went out so that it would be shown that they all are not of us" (1 John 2:19).

If we embrace His divine character, we will be adept to stand firm in our faith and know that the presence and power of God are still with us because we're not in this alone. He will be with us as we labor for more of His ways, and know that His grace will suffice to get us through (2 Cor 12:9–10). And this undeniable pursuit will generate a daily life of His presence that will get us through the most challenging days and prepare us for tomorrow and the future. Who would not aspire to pursue this, especially in today's cultural movement? Even during the evilness—that is so prevalent in this society, the Almighty One is still in our midst; He has not eluded us. His Word and Spirit are within the clasp of our hearts and minds; because He needs you and me to cling to all His ways of holiness, living out a life of purity (Ps 119:1–16). Regardless of the looming days we're experiencing—this is our time to shine for Him!

It is as critical now more than ever that we grab and hold on to all of God's guidelines of holiness in our daily life with every bit of spiritual strength. We must nurture our Christian lives, develop spiritual change, accelerate our growth, increase our faith, and obtain a more desirable and pleasing life for our Heavenly Father. Signs of embracing Jesus Christ in our daily practices will indicate our genuine commitment to Him.

When someone truly embraces God's holiness, they cling to living as Jesus Christ did, defending the faith at all costs, supportive and content with His plans for their life, accepting His will no matter what, adopting and clasping to

His word enthusiastically, and champion the guidance of the Holy Spirit. This type of "embracing" is one kind of love for Jesus Christ that is second to none, treasuring Him above all things in life! 1 John 5:3.

John Wycliffe, a philosopher, preacher, and reformer in the Middle Ages, spent a lifetime promoting the truth of God's word and opposed any other authority that spoke otherwise. He embraced the validity of Scripture and was committed to telling as many people as he could about the truth of the Bible. Wycliffe was more persuaded by Romans 1:17: "*The righteousness of God is revealed from faith for faith, as it is written, 'The righteous shall live by faith.'* In other words, the only way to be saved and "be right with God" was through faith in Jesus Christ alone.

As he studied the Scriptures, he recognized the corruption within the Catholic Church and called for church reform. He rejected the practice of indulgences and said this of salvation, "Trust wholly in Christ; rely altogether on his sufferings; beware of seeking to be justified in any other way than by his righteousness." Wycliffe held similar views regarding salvation to those of Martin Luther nearly 150 years later. Thus, he is known as the "Morning Star to the Reformation." As he did so diligently, John Wycliffe lit the way for many believers to embrace, follow and live by these truths today. [1] This is one great example for us to follow in these times we're facing today.

1. Insight for Living, "John Wycliffe."

Final Steps

Enforce Holiness

Why is God's most divine nature required and needs to be implemented in the lives of Christians today?

1. Because God demands it in our lives, and it's His will for us to be holy. 1 Thess 4:3–8.

2. If Jesus Christ is our daily model, we must imitate His life because it marks our real identity and purpose as Christians. 1 Cor 11:1, Eph 5:1–2.

3. It sets us apart from the world and unto our Lord for His purpose of service in this life. 2 Timothy chapter 2; "Be a Good Soldier for Jesus Christ."

When we embrace this most needed attribute in our everyday life, it will force you and me, in time, to come to terms with this reality; "True Christianity is a fight." One of the most profound stories of God's holiness is probably of the greatest prophet in history, Isaiah. In Isaiah 6:1–8, we see a time when this significant prophet would witness the power of God's holiness when the angels sang out a beautiful chorus song that shook the Temple to its foundations, "Holy, Holy, Holy is the Lord Almighty!" Then Isaiah realized he was not worthy of being in God's presence. Can you imagine every Christian so on fire for the holiness of God in their lives that it would rock the foundations of this corrupt world?

It was important for Isaiah to see the holiness of God because it would reveal what separated him from His Creator: his sinfulness. He knew he was a sinful man before God with no hope of measuring up to God's standard of purity and righteousness. But at that moment, seraphim touched his lips with burning coal and told him his guilt had been removed. It was not the hot burning coal that cleansed him; it was a Holy God! This excruciating cleansing was necessary before Isaiah could fulfill the task that God had set before him. Because it was after this purification that Isaiah realized his calling from God; at that moment, the great prophet stated these powerful words: "Lord, I'll go! Send me!" And today, this attitude is needed in our homes, churches, and communities.

When we look at this powerful story of Isaiah, we see a faithful and loyal man dedicated to His Lord, who was willing to go and send a profound message of conviction to the Israelites. And just like today in our country, this was in a time that was considered one of the most unstable periods in Jerusalem's history, from both a political and religious point of view.

At the beginning of his ministry, Isaiah was well-liked. But over time, he became unfavorable when his message was so difficult for the people to hear. Why? Because he was called to tell the people to turn from their lives of sin and warn them of God's impending judgment and punishment. Isaiah's purpose was to bring back the nation of Judah (God's nation) to faithfulness and proclaim the coming of the Savior and His future reign. He sends the message to Judah and Israel of condemnation, hope, and salvation through the coming of the Messiah, Jesus Christ.

And no matter the instability and turmoil between man and the nation, Isaiah never wavered from His complete dedication to God. He was committed to sending a message to the people that they needed to hear God's word and turn away from their sinful ways of living. His ministry and service to the Lord stretched over half a century, and it's said that King Manasseh martyred him. No matter the consequences the evil world threw his way, Isaiah would serve his time for Yahweh.

Even great and faithful men in the Old Testament, such as Moses, Gideon and David, acknowledged their unrighteousness in contrast to the righteousness and holiness of God. They realized the need for Him in their daily lives. As a result, their repentant prayers gained great power and effectiveness in their lives as great examples for us today.

If we look at some of the major themes of Paul's, James, John's, and Peter's letters in the New Testament, they constantly battled to spread the Good News and defend their faith. Still, their relentless mission and service were always intact because they knew there was a need for God's holiness in the lives of so many. After all, it would lead people to 1) repent and turn away from their sins to a Holy Lord, 2) rely upon the Truth of God's grace, mercy, and love, 3) accept Jesus Christ by faith as Savior and Lord, 4) live under the freedom of Christ and not the law, 5) realize and understand that the word of God brings clarity and truth, 6) recognize warning signs against unholiness, 7) be steadfast and firm in the faith, 8) become Doers of the Word, 9) learn how to endure and persevere, 10) faithfully serve out of Christlike love, 11) strive for a Christ-centered life, and 12) and long to live a life that honors a Holy God! This ongoing process of sanctification sets us apart as righteous ones unto a Holy Lord, and we can only succeed in this by applying God's word with the help of the Holy Spirit.

While the world wants to support and endorse more acts of immorality, our Lord wants you and me to champion and further God's holiness (like the Disciples) in an ailing society that's dying spiritually. And a powerful takeaway is this; our holy life causes people around us to glorify God (1 Pet 2:9–12). So, is our pursuit of God's divine character needed and worth it in this last ditched effort on earth? Yes, every day, one step at a time! When we allow the Holy Spirit to fine-tune our life in Christ and put that in motion, it will separate our wants and needs from the pleasures of unrighteousness into a driving force for more of His ways.

As we grow in our journey with the Lord, "God's holy people will do whatever it takes to remove those things that are disabling their walk with the Lord." But in this all-out attempt, the enemy will do whatever it takes to deter and distract us from the beauty of God's plan. We need to ingrain this into our minds and hearts when it comes to the work of the enemy; he's out to lead us down a destructive path of continual defiance and disobedience, which is enough to break down any system of holiness.

If we're going to make a difference in this world, we must be on the front-line of God's holiness, ready to put it on active display. His divine nature is evident in our lives when we are obedient to His word and living it out—and that's when we're of practical use to our Lord.

Just like Saul (who became the great apostle Paul), he was out to perse-cute all Christians. He was an enemy of the Lord and was of no service to God because he was far from His presence. But once he became a bondservant of Christ Jesus, called to be an apostle, he was set apart for the gospel of God, and then he was of practical use for God's glory!

The identification mark for Paul was this. He longed for, loved, and dedicated himself to complete service for His Lord, and he knew Who ac-complished that work of righteousness in his life! At one stage in Paul's life, his actions were the opposite of Christ, but his one choice to surrender to the working of God's grace made all the difference in the world. And that right decision connected him with the Lord, and it would impact millions of people's lives for centuries! And this is the divine connection we need today as believers!

In the 1720s, it only took one man on the frontline who was astounded and shocked by the deadness of the church. He would take it upon himself to enforce the Truth of the Scriptures to his own church. He preached the need for conversion and a life-changing commitment back to Christ. This profoundly influenced other men and led them to preach the power of God's word to their churches as well. This movement would see people give their lives to Jesus Christ, repent for their lawless acts, and avoid the worldly lust that would succumb to their lives. They, in turn, would have a higher regard for the word of God and live a life that reflected more of His divine nature. Because of the people's hearts desiring more of God's ways, the Spirit began to set in, revival grew, and a generation was transformed.

What took place during this era is said to be the most intense, dramatic, and explosive spiritual movement of God on American soil. It is estimated that one-tenth of the entire population of the American colonies was converted, and over 300 churches on fire for the holiness of God were planted. To put this conversion into a powerful perspective, it is estimated that the population of the thirteen colonies during the first Great Awakening was about 2.3 million, meaning 230,000 new believers came to know Christ.

Today, about 340 million people live in the United States. And if we were to see the same fruitful results in an Awakening today, that would equate to approximately 34 million new Christians! Wow! And to put that number into a more robust scope that would equal nearly every person in Texas, Alaska, North and South Dakota, Rhode Island, and Wyoming who would come to accept Jesus Christ as Lord of their lives!

And here was the key. Dedicated men of God stood at the forefront of this great movement in the 18th century, just like others in the late 18th century. Another example was during the Jesus Movement and Revolution in the 1960 and 70s; they carried out the truth at all costs. They did not hold back on preaching man's absolute dependence on God, the only way we can glorify our Creator. Instead, they iterated man's justification by faith in a Savior and the need to turn to a God that could provide them with a life of eternity.

But out of these Great Awakenings was a fiery buzz for more of God's holiness, bringing spiritual restoration. These awakenings impacted people's lives throughout generations, and they made their impression and marks of spiritual enhancement and advancement, which led people to Jesus Christ. It all started with faithful and obedient individuals who chose to make an impact for the Kingdom of God. Any devout follower can affect a society and culture if they choose to glorify God!

Jesus reminds us in Matt 12:34 that in examining a man's heart, we can learn what kind of man he is, and Jesus says it is from the overflow of a man's heart that he speaks. With that, it is from Isaiah's writings that we learn of his unswerving and undeniable faithfulness and his complete humility before a

Sovereign God. We also see in his book that he surrounded himself with men of godly and holy living (just like the men of the first Great Awakening). They did not get entangled with men of the corrupt nation that was so prevailing during their times. A key takeaway is this; "What we place in our heart, mind, and body will filter out its desired results, whether holy or unholy.

The differentiator is this; Paul describes himself as "pressing on" toward the goal of Christlikeness (Phil 3:13–14). And that's pushing through all the barriers, and pursuing God's holiness, no matter what. Even Peter reminds us in his second Epistle chapter one that God has given us every resource for living a godly life; in other words, there are no excuses. Our pursuit of God's ways is our "real life" in Christ—that vital union and togetherness with Him.

But despite all the negative news and battles we'll face in this ongoing mission, there is Great News! Our Almighty God has already pre-thought, predestined, and preset you and me so we can still progress through sanctification on this Earth because of our steadfast faith in Him! Indeed, God's patience, mercy, grace, and love are immeasurable and will help us overcome these difficult days if we pursue and enforce His most essential nature. Therefore, if applied, the PowerPoint of God's holiness will lead us to these beautiful experiences below if we implement it in our daily lives:

- Establishes a closer relationship with our Lord. Jas 4:8.

- Engages us more effectively with the Holy Spirit. 1 Cor 3:16.

- Enables us to discern right from wrong and good from evil. Isa 5:20.

- Exposes our sinful nature to the point of repentance. John 16:8.

- Endure and persevere through these turbulent times. 1 Pet 5:10.

- Enhances our hope in a Loving and Holy Creator. Isa 40:31.

- Encourages our faith more and even affects others around us. 1 John 5:14.

- Excels us from a state of complacency to spiritual growth. Eph 4:11–17.

- Elevates our maturity and sanctification stages. 2 Pet 1:3–8.

- Enriches our lives with spiritual blessings. Eph 1:3.

- Enlivens our prayer life. Matt 21:22, Heb 4:16, Phil 4:6–7.

- Embrace and accept God's will. 2 Cor 5:17.

- Expectation and hope of an extraordinary life He has in store for us. Col 1:5.

- Enjoyment of tasting His goodness and lovingkindness. Ps118:1–4.

- Empowers our heart, soul, mind, and strength. Col 1:11, Eph 3:16–17.

It should be our #1 goal to strive for Christlikeness, excel, and rise above the mediocre state like Isaiah and the men of the Great Awakenings. The ways of this world should never be commonplace for Christians—because this is not our final resting place. God's word reminds us in Matt 5: 3, 8, 48, "God blesses those who are poor and realize their need for him, for the Kingdom of Heaven is theirs" . . . "God blesses those whose hearts are pure, for they will see God," and "But you are to be perfect, even as your Father in Heaven is perfect. "And the gut punch for you and me is this; we are to present our bodies as a living and Holy sacrifice, one that is acceptable unto God, which is our credible service" (Rom 12:1). Here's an excellent motivation for us to think about in our daily life; when this life is over, we will be presented Holy and unblameable in His sight (Col 1:22).

Once again, Peter reminds us in his first epistle that, as God's chosen ones, we're to live a holy life in this unholy world. We're told to abstain from the evil things that rage war against our souls. He implores us to be righteous and faithful to the sacred ways of God so the unbelieving world will see our honorable behavior. Then they will give honor to God when He judges the world. Peter tells us in his second epistle to pay attention to the Scriptures and stand by the truth it teaches.

While the world craves, pushes, and interjects more acts of lawlessness into this society, we counter this by enforcing holy living into our daily lives. Always remember that living a life pleasing to God will reap spiritual blessings! And what a reward! Seek it, embrace it, and enforce it for His glory today!

Isa 45:4–7, "And why have I called you for this work? Why did I call you by name when you did not know me? It is for the sake of Jacob my servant, Israel my chosen one. I am the LORD; there is no other God. I have equipped you for battle, though you don't even know me, so all the world from east to west will know there is no other God. I am the LORD, and there is no other. I create the light and make the darkness. I send good times and bad times. I, the LORD, am the one who does these things."

And the good news is recorded in Rev 21:1–4, "Then I saw a new Heaven and a new earth, for the old Heaven and the old Earth had disappeared. And the sea was also gone. And I saw the holy city, the new Jerusalem, coming down from God out of Heaven like a bride beautifully dressed for her husband. I heard a loud shout from the throne, saying, "Look, God's home is now among his people! He will live with them, and they will be his people. God himself will be with them. He will wipe every tear from their eyes, and there will be no more death or sorrow or crying or pain. All these things are gone forever."

Glossary

A

Abandoned — deserted, forsaken, cast aside, unused, *but you are never stranded in Christ!*

Able — *capable and qualified to have the power, skill, and means to work for the Lord!*

Abundance — large quantity, mass, *extremely abundant life as a believer in Jesus.*

Acceptance — receive something suitable, approved, *welcoming His Word in your life.*

Access —a means of entering a place – *your entrance into Heaven as a believer in Christ.*

Accomplish —achieve, complete, fulfill, finish, and conclude *our victory in Jesus Christ.*

Accountable —responsible, bound to, liable, *we are to blame and will be held!*

Accused —charged with a crime, charges against the guilty, *but in Christ, you are innocent.*

Acknowledge —*accept the truth of God's word, bow to it, and address it in your life.*

Action —doing something, aim towards, *steps and efforts taken to know our Lord more.*

Admit —*acknowledge, profess, and confess that Jesus Christ is Lord of your life.*

Advantage —*once we surrender to Christ — there's new life in Him, sins forgiven, transformed, power of His indwelling Spirit at work in us, faithful servants, eternal life.*

Advice —*guidance, recommendation, direction, and pointers provided in God's word.*

Affection —*a gentle fondness of love, endearment, and friendship we can have with Christ.*

Agape Love —the highest form of love, *the love of God for man, and of man for God.*

Agreement —*in harmony, accordance, and agreeing with God's ways in your life.*

Aim —*work towards, set sights on, pursue, strive for, and target Christlikeness.*

Alert —*readiness for action, discerning towards a threat or danger that could be harmful.*

Align —*arrange your life in an order that positions and sets you toward Christlikeness.*

Alliance —*a union for mutual benefit, a bonded association with Christ in your life.*

Almighty —absolute overall and unlimited Power in all things —*nothing compares to God.*

Allows —approve of, pleased with, invest, entrust, *yield to, and acknowledge His ways.*

Alone —the state of no one present in your life, singleness. *But as Christians, we know that He's always there.*

Alter —is a structure upon which offerings such as sacrifices are made for religious purposes—a place for consecration. *Our hearts are an invisible altar where the war between the flesh and the spirit rages. When we surrender areas of our lives to the control of the Holy Spirit, we are, in effect, laying that area on the altar before God.*

Alternative —*available as another opportunity of relief, like accepting Christ as Savior.*

Ambition —a fervent desire to achieve something, intention, purpose, *a goal to serve God.*

Anew —a new, different, and typically more positive way, *a fresh new beginning in Him.*

Anger —a strong feeling of hostility and rage, *but in Christ, He can provide self—control.*

Ambition —a powerful desire to achieve something, *an intent to know and grow in Christ.*

Anointed —chosen for a position, and *once in Christ, you are His candidate for service.*

Anxiety —is a reaction to a stressful situation, but God's word comforts us.

Apart —separated away from, distant, far away, *cut off, let go for good — done.*

Apostasy —the abandonment, betrayal, defection, and desertion of faith — *spiritual doom.*

Apparent —clearly visible, understood, plain, striking, recognizable, *manifest Godliness.*

Apply —make an effort, use, exercise, put into practice, and *show commitment to His word.*

Appointed —specified, determined, allotted, assigned, *designated, chosen for His glory.*

Approval —to be honest and trustworthy, having a positive and *favorable opinion of Him in us.*

Arrogance —attitude of superiority, *extreme sense of one's importance, spiritually weak.*

Ashamed —embarrassed, guilty because of an action, *one choice for Christ removes it all.*

Ask —*call for, seek for His counsel, beg, and crave for His direction and guidance.*

Assumption —accepted as accurate without proof, *God's word is precept upon precept.*

Atonement —*restitution, satisfying a wrongdoing, reconciling with God through Jesus.*

Attempt —do your best, strive, make every effort, and give your *all to the Lord.*

Attention —*take notice, away, observe, regard as in paying attention to the Scripture.*

Attitude —way of thinking, perspective, approach, your feelings — *good or bad?*

Authority —*the power of the right to give orders in our life, such as God's word in us.*

Awe —*reverential respect, admiration, wonder, and amazement in all God has done!*

B

Balance —*stability, steadiness, and footing in daily life, such as God's word at work.*

Barren —too poor to produce, unfruitful, *but fruitfulness can be abundant in Christ.*

Barrier —an obstacle that prevents movement or access, a hurdle, *a spiritual roadblock.*

Basics —*the essential facts, principles, and realities of God's word active in us daily.*

Behavior —one's conduct, actions, practices, manners, ways, *habits — pure or impure?*

Benefit —*an advantage or profit gained, such as our eternal inheritance in Christ.*

Bind —*tied, fastened together, shackled, and secured in Christ once we believe in Him.*

Bitterness —*anger and resentment that can be removed once a believer in Christ.*

Blame —*one held accountable, condemnation, accused, but in Christ, you're forgiven.*

Blameless —innocent of wrongdoing, free from blame, *faultless in God's eyes as His.*

Blasphemy —the unforgivable sin, ungodliness, disrespect, unholy, *but the Lord forgives.*

Belief —an acceptance that a statement is true, *free from doubt in who you are in Christ.*

Believer —one who believes *something is effective, a follower and disciple of Christ.*

Birth – *Spiritual* —*one who has been born into the family of God and craves fellowship with other believers — and a desire to grow, develop and mature in Christlikeness.*

Blessed —our well-being and *the full impact of God's presence in our lives.*

Blessings —*God's favor, goodness, goodwill, and happiness in our lives.*

Blindness —poor perception, *inability to see anything spiritually impure or hurtful.*

Blood of Christ —*sacrificial death and complete atoning work of Jesus on our behalf.*

Boasting —excessively proud, self-satisfied about oneself – *no place in God's house.*

Body of Christ —*collection and unity of true believers in a place of service and praising Christ.*

Boldness —willingness – the quality of a solid and clear appearance, *fearless for God.*

Breath of Life —the life and power of God, given to man to operate him, get him going, set him in motion, but the key lies in this – *who controls our on and off button?*

Burdensome —challenging to carry out or fulfill; only *with God's help can we persevere.*

Business of God —*managing and stewardship of God's ways for His purpose and plan.*

Busyness —many things to do *that can lead to a disconnection from God.*

C

Calamity —an event causing significant distress, affliction, crisis, adversity, or *temporary setback.*

Calculating —scheming, ruthless behavior, self-interest, *driven by the flesh than spirit.*

Calling —a strong urge toward a particular way of life, mission, or *course of action for God.*

Callous —insensitive, cruel disregard for others, cold-hearted, the heart of stone, *not of God.*

Carelessness —failure to give *attention to God* in an area that could avoid harm or errors.

Caring —*a kindhearted and genuine concern for all people in a Christlike fashion.*

Chance —the possibility of something happening, *an opportunity, and hope to make it right.*

Change —different, converted, transformed, *a Godly make-over for His glory.*

Character —personality, attributes, *identity, qualities, the uniqueness of Christ in us.*

Choice —select, decide, option, course of action, solution, *way out from the bad to good.*

Chosen —*selected, fitting, suitable, called for, expected, preferred by God for His glory.*

Christian —*one who believes in, professes, and follows all the ways of Jesus Christ.*

Christianity —*belief in the teachings of Christ's life, death, and resurrection, Good News.*

Christlike —the result of Christian growth and maturity, *exemplifying behaviors of Christ.*

Church —*The Body* — *all who have placed their faith in Jesus Christ for salvation.*

Citizenship —*citizens of Heaven on earth with our eternal resting place in His Kingdom.*

Clarity —apparent, simple, plain, understandable; *there is no confusion in God's word. It's crystal clear.*

Cleansing —intent to clean something thoroughly, purify *Christ, can wash away our sins.*

Cling —*grasp, clench, grip, hold onto "tightly" all of God's ways for your life.*

Clothing *Spiritually* —indicates spiritual character developed by submission to God. *Christians are to "put on the Lord Jesus Christ " like a garment representing a Christ—covered life and, as a result, character consistent with God's way of life.*

Comfort —a state of ease, freedom from pain, *a reassurance of God's peace in us.*

Comfort Zone —behavioral state of anxiety control, *lack of spiritual growth.*

Command —authoritative order, instruct, charge, *require, prescribed from God.*

Commitment —*dedicated, devoted, faithful, attentive to a cause for our good — His glory.*

Communication —*God communicates to us through His word, and we talk to Him in prayer.*

Community —*a body that loves Jesus Christ and fellowships and supports each other.*

Communion —*sharing intimate thoughts, remembering what Christ did for us.*

Compare —contrast, differentiates —the difference between, side by side, *flesh vs. spirit?*

Compelled —forced, pressured, or *an obligation to do something like living out His word.*

Complacent —self-satisfied, proud, pleased with self, careless, lazy, *spiritually flawed.*

Complainer —dissatisfaction, grumbler, moaner, whiner, find fault, *spiritually toxic.*

Completion —*the fulfillment, fruition, and his successful work in us until Glory.*

Compromise —agreement, settled, trade-off, cooperate, give-and-take— *God or world?*

Condemnation —extreme disapproval of, *but there is no condemnation if you belong to Jesus Christ.*

Confessions —admitting guilt, owning up, being accountable, professing, exposing, *a Godly act.*

Confidence —a belief that we can rely on another, *a firm trust like our position with Christ.*

Confirm —*establish correctness,* discover, determine, grasp, take in, and *cling to His Truths.*

Conflict —a dispute that can lead to discord and division —*so often, it is the work of Satan.*

Conform —comply with rules, abide by, obey, agree to, fulfill, respect, and *stick to God.*

Confusion —*lack of understanding*, uncertainty, doubt, hesitancy, *the enemy at work.*

Connection —relationship, *linked together, relevant, relatable, bonded with the Lord.*

Conscience is awareness and knowledge of right and wrong; the *key for believers is applying God's word.*

Consecrate —*as true believers; our lives are a living sacrifice to Him, separated from evil.*

Consequences —a result or effect of an action or outcome *could be dire.*

Consistent —*done the same way over time, accurate, no variation from God's word.*

Consuming —devour, take, feast on, engaging, deeply felt, *filling our minds with Him.*

Contentment —happiness, satisfaction, pleasure, comfort, *gratified with His provisions.*

Contrary —opposite and inconsistent, *such as the ways of the world vs. God's ways.*

Contrast —*strikingly different; as believers in Christ, we are unlike anything in this world.*

Conversation —a talk between people the Lord welcomes from us daily.

Conviction —declaring someone guilty, *a position that can be made right once in Christ.*

Cooperate —work jointly towards the same result *with God every day.*

Correction —making something right, rectifying, *all cleared up when we accept Christ!*

Corruption —dishonesty, deception, wrongdoing, *misconduct that is not a life in Christ.*

Counsel —advice, guidance, direction, *enlightenment facts from His Spirit for our good.*

Covenant —a binding agreement, a *life-or-death agreement between two — you and God.*

Craftsmen —God gives talent and ability to specific individuals to carry out His work to its completion. *To conduct His designs with success and* an element of excellence and success in their works; we all have that capacity through the Holy Spirit.

Creation —completeness, totality, fulfillment, or perfection – *God's awesomeness.*

Creator —Someone Who brings something *into existence and sustains it—God at work.*

Credibility —trustworthy, character, dependable, *reputation of a Godly person.*

Cross —*the intersection of God's love and His justice. For believers in Christ's sacrifice, it's being dead to self and following Jesus wholeheartedly.*

Crown —*an honor received for our good and faithful works and a cause for boundless joy.*

Crucial —critical to the success or failure of something, significant, *game-changer.*

Cunning —having skill in achieving one's end; deceptive, crafty, *scheming, not good.*

Curtain —divided the two sacred rooms of the Tabernacle — the Holy Place and Most Holy Place. It symbolizes how people were separated from God because of sin. Thanks to Christ, this curtain has been ripped, and we now have access to the Father because of what Christ did for us on the cross.

D

Danger —the possibility of suffering or harm, hazard, risk, or *instability when not in Christ.*

Darkness —partial or total absence of light, gloom, *dullness, void, and blackness.*

Death —the end of physical life, *but as believers in Christ, spiritual life continues forever.*

Deceive —causing one to believe *what is untrue, mislead, fool, cheat, double-crosser.*

Decision —a resolution, settled, and *final when you accept Christ as Lord.*

Declines —refuse to take advantage of, turn down, pass up, *could change your life.*

Dedication is setting apart or consecrating things to God, devoted to a holy purpose by a Divine Being.

Defiance —open resistance, bold disobedience, *disregard, rebellious —be careful.*

Delight —*please someone significantly, what the Lord desires from us daily.*

Delivered —the deliverance of God's people from sin and guilt, God's supremacy over the Egyptian deities.

Demand —insistent request, an order, ultimatum, urge, stipulation, *challenge to get right.*

Demonstrate —show how something is done, display, illustrate, and *exemplify His qualities.*

Depend —*controlled by, rely on, be based on, rest, and lean on God for all things.*

Depraved —corrupt, wicked, lead astray, poison another, defile, infect – *not of God.*

Desires —want, yearning, longing, craving, *eagerness, enthusiasm to know God more.*

Despair —*complete loss or absence of hope,* unhappiness, discouragement, depression.

Desperate —feeling hopeless at one's end, *but not in Christ, for you are anew.*

Destroy —put an end to, damage, tear down, break up, devastate, *enemy's goal.*

Determined —made a firm decision, resolved *not to change when you accept Christ.*

Develop —form, grow, more mature, *flourish, blossom, succeed in all His ways.*

Devise —think up, develop, formulate, design, and *plan to know God more.*

Devour —consume, gorge oneself, gobble up — *things we should do with God's word.*

Difficult —need effort and skill to achieve, weary, brutal, *without God's —it is impossible.*

Diligence —persistent effort, attention to detail, continuance, *an intent to please Him.*

Disadvantage —*an unfavorable circumstance, a defect, or a liability that could be costly.*

Disagree —a different opinion, fail to agree, challenge, argue, quarrel, *be careful.*

Discernment —*God-gifted ability to judge well, wise, sharp, insightful, so needed today.*

Discontent —dissatisfaction, lack of contentment, a sense of grievance; it's *spiritually crippling.*

Discourage —cause someone to lose confidence, enthusiasm, *not a Christlike attribute.*

Disobedience —failure or refusal to obey rules or God's authority.

Distract —prevent from giving full attention to something. It's a state of disturbance and confusion; it's the *devil's work.*

Disposition— *"Spiritually"* —*how we respond to life and, most importantly, God. Our response to Him should be essential in our minds daily.*

Divine —*Godly, Godlike, Saintly, Spiritual, Heavenly, Holy; it's God's ways.*

Division —the act of separating, breaking up, splitting, severing, *disconnecting from the bad to good.*

Doer —*takes an active part, does not just think about it, "achieving God's directives."*

Doubt —connotes the idea of weakness in faith, negative attitude, or action *— not of God.*

E

Effective —successful in producing the desired result, valuable, *such as our walk with God.*

Effort —a vigorous or determined attempt, endeavor, an *all-out exertion to serve Him.*

Elevate —*raise and lift up that higher position you possess in Christ — every day.*

Embrace —hold closely in one's arms, clasp to, enclose, and *entwine oneself around the Lord.*

Emotions —a natural state of mind, feeling, sensation, *reaction or response, passion for?*

Emptiness —contain nothing, worthless, ineffective, *once wholly in Christ— you are filled.*

Encourage —*supporter, confidence or hope to one, uplift, helpful, a Christlike enforcer.*

Endurance —tolerance, bearing, patience, acceptance, persistence, *a staying power in Him.*

Engage —become involved, participate in, embark on, and *play a key role in all His ways.*

Enhance —*intensify, increase, and further improve the quality of your walk with the Lord.*

Enlightenment —learning, development, insight, *and advancement in God's ways.*

Enslaved —a cause to someone losing their freedom of choice or action. Christ can release us from any bondage and give us freedom forever when He chooses life in Him.

Enthusiasm —intense and eager enjoyment, *nothing like a relationship with Jesus Christ.*

Envy —jealousy, covet, bitterness, resentment, a wrong desire, *a sinful vice that cripples.*

Equality —a state of being equal, *fair, and impartial; we are all created by God equally.*

Error —a mistake, oversight, misinterpretation, *a misconception, but God can fix it.*

Establish —set up, start, begin, get going, and *bring into being your intended life for Him.*

Everlasting —forever, without end, imperishable, immortal, deathless – *priceless.*

Evidence —proof, confirms, reveals, displays, manifests, and *signifies your identity in Christ.*

Evil —wicked, harmful, corrupt, immoral, sin —*life or death matter.*

Exalt —hold someone in high regard, *glorify, praise, worship, and reverence to the Holy One.*

Example —*characteristic of its kind, illustrating one's case, a representative for Christ.*

Excitement —a *feeling of great enthusiasm and eagerness as you grow closer to the Lord.*

Exclusive —complete, total, whole, absolute, *your undivided attention to the Lord.*

Excuse —seek to justify, rationalize, overlook, disregard, or *ignore the Good News.*

Exodus —a mass departure of people, God's great deliverance for His children in bondage.

Expectation —the belief that something will happen, anticipation, the *outlook for our good.*

Experience —valuable contact, acquaintance, exposure to, and *understanding of Him in you.*

F

Failure —lack of success, unfulfilling, *but as a true child of God, you have not failed.*

Faith —complete trust, confidence, hopefulness, belief, *dependence upon His word.*

Faithfulness —unfailing loyalty to someone, *consistently putting into practice His ways.*

Faithless —disloyal, unfaithful, unreliable, *even though we are faithless, God's faithful.*

Fatalism —the belief that all events are inevitable *and out of God's control. It debilitates faith.*

Favor —gaining approval, acceptance, pleasure, or *unique benefits or blessings from Him.*

Fear —terror, alarm, anxiety, worry, uneasiness, distress, doubt, dread, *spiritual weakness.*

Feel —awareness, sense, discern, *conscious of something powerful at work in us.*

Find —discover, realize, become aware, appear, show, and *manifest His word in us.*

Fixated —*obsessed with, gripped by, devoted to, focused — as we should be as* Christians.

Flee —run away from danger, escape, leave, get out quickly, *spiritually discerning.*

Flesh —*the part of a believer who disagrees with the Spirit — cannot coexist.*

Filth —foul, disgusting dirt, contamination, and garbage—is *not a spiritual virtue.*

Focus —the *center of interest, focal point, backbone, anchor,* the *basis of the Controlling One in our lives.*

Follower —*a devoted person to a cause, companion, admirer, supporter, lover of Christ.*

Fool —acting unwisely, imprudent, idiot, *a halfwit not taking God's word seriously.*

Foothold —*an issue of who influences the heart. Is it the Lord or the enemy? A place where you can put your foot safely and securely when climbing like the Rock.*

Footstool —is a symbol of lowliness, humility, and unimportance—*selflessness.*

Forgetfulness —lose the remembrance of, forget facts; God's *word is a fresh reminder daily.*

Forgiveness —absolute forgiving, cleared, pardon, *God's mercy on us as sinners.*

Foundation —starting point, heart, principle, fundamentals, cornerstone, *Godly position.*

Freedom —*the power, right, and privilege we possess to speak of the Good News of Christ.*

Fruit of the Spirit —*Holy Spirit's presence, working in the lives of true maturing believers.*

Fruitfulness —*is beneficial for the work of the Lord in our daily lives for His Glory.*

Fulfill —bring to completion, succeed, and *bring about His good fruit in your daily life.*

Futile —incapable of producing valid results, pointless, *but His Spirit in us can have.*

G

Genealogy —historical facts in the Bible, the importance of family to God, proof of prophecies.

Generosity is the Christlike quality of genuine kindness, honor, and lack of *prejudice.*

Gentleness —*supreme kindness, mild-mannered, tender, softness, courteous, considerate.*

Genuine —someone authentic, honest, legit, sound, sterling, *rightful in all His ways.*

Gifts —given willingly, a present, offering, favor, inheritance, *bestowal from Him to us.*

Giving —handing over freely, *God's children providing others with what He is gifted us.*

Glorify —praise, exalt, worship, reverence, adore, honor, bless, *magnify Him in all we do.*

Glory —*splendor, holiness, and majesty of God, a place of unfathomable praise and honor.*

Goal —a future desired result to achieve something *as Citizens of Heaven on Earth.*

God —*All Supreme Being, Creator, Who is Perfect in Power, Wisdom, and Goodness.*

Godly Fear —*a reverent feeling to God, a deterrent to sin, and brings us closer to God.*

God's Fairness —*living under God's righteousness and justness — love, grace, and mercy.*

God's Kingdom —the rule of an eternal, sovereign God over all the universe.

God's Laws —His unchangeable divine nature, expression of love, joy, holy, just, pleasing.

God's Nature —*All Supreme — Holy, Just, Righteous, All Omni, Loving Kind Creator.*

God's Presence —*always present in believers by His Spirit*— *a strong relationship.*

God's Promises —*to help strengthen our faith* and have something to hold on to.

God's Protection —*Heaven is our home—we are spiritually safe as believers in Christ.*

God's Season —*appointed time for all seasons of life* — *part of living out God's plan.*

God's Timing —*when all falls comfortably, naturally into place* — *in His appointed time.*

God's View —*God always sees how everything works together to conform us to His image.*

God's Will is things that align *with God's superior and supreme plan and purpose.*

God's Word —the infallible *Truth, Righteous, and Goodness of all God's Holy ways.*

God's Work —*where we are equipped with His gift to benefit others and accomplish His good works in love and faithfulness* — *with His guidance* — *representing Him.*

Godliness —*the practice, exercise, and discipline of devoutness to God's word.*

Good —satisfactory, acceptable, high quality, and standard, *up to His mark.*

Goodness —*Godly virtue, integrity, honesty, truthfulness, honorable, righteousness, caring.*

Gossiper —betrayal of confidence, a perverse person stirring up dissension, *not Godly.*

Grace —*God's favor towards the unworthy, His goodwill, generosity, and lovingkindness.*

Gratitude —*the Godly quality of thankfulness, appreciation, recognition, credit, and respect.*

Greed —a selfish desire for something, most often worldly things — *not God.*

Growth —*the increasing, maturing, thriving, and sprouting of Christlikeness in us.*

Guide — *"One" who shows the way to others and gives advice to resolve life's problems.*

Guilt —committed a crime or wrongdoing but *cleared when accepting Christ as Savior.*

H

Habits —a regular practice or custom that is hard to give up, *maybe a spiritual detriment.*

Half—heartedness —no enthusiasm or energy, *not "all in" — wholeheartedly for the Lord.*

Happiness —the feeling of joy and satisfaction that *we should experience daily as Christians.*

Hardheartedness —incapable of being moved to pity or tenderness, *no Christlike value.*

Harmony —in tune simultaneously, sounds *joined into whole units—as one.*

Harvest—Spiritual —*users of our gifts in God's field to reap what we sow, a sign of growth.*

Hatred —intense dislike or ill will, *a poison that can destroy our spirit from within.*

Healing —the process of becoming sound or healthy – *spiritually eased and relieved.*

Health —*a continual spiritual treatment and nourishment of our heart, mind, and soul.*

Heaven —physical reality beyond earth—*the spiritual reality where God lives, where we can also live as believers in Jesus Christ—forever.*

Heavenly Father —First person of the Trinity – *Supreme Being, Creator, and Sustainer.*

Hear —get, listen to, *discern, be informed,* told, made aware of, *given to understand Him.*

Heart —*the central part and core of our spiritual makeup in thoughts, actions, and words.*

Heart Set —*modeling the force of what is controlling the heart to the outside world! It is either glorifying God or not.*

Heed —pay attention to take notice of, consider, *give ear to observe, and apply His ways.*

Hell —the total, conscious, eternal separation from God's blessings, *so choose Christ.*

Helper —one that helps, aids, or assists, *a Christlike assistant out of genuine love.*

Holiness is God's most divine nature and characteristic, which is the goal of all human moral character. It is a disposition of being separate from the ways of the world and required to be in God's Almighty presence.

Holy Spirit —the third person of the Trinity, Comforter, Counselor — *God in action in our life.*

Honesty —*moral correctness, high principles, right-mindedness, worthiness, Godly truth.*

Honor —high respect, esteem, distinction, privilege, respect, *notable to the True God.*

Hope —expectation for a sure thing to happen, *longing for a great outcome.*

Hopelessness —absolute despair, no hope, a feeling of loss, but hope is alive and well in Christ.

Hospitality —the *Christlike quality* of friendly and *generous reception of all people.*

Humility —*Christlike modesty, a low view of oneself, lack of pride, Godly meekness.*

I

Idolatry —*worship of idols other than God, ungodliness, and unholy in the eyes of God.*

Ignore —refuse to notice, *disregard, leave out, disobey, defy.* [insert sad face]

Image —a representation of the external form, likeness, resemblance, portrayal – *Godly.*

Imitator —one who copies the behavior of another, a person *in high esteem — Jesus Christ.*

Immaturity —not growing, *a "spiritual infant" looks and acts like a human infant.*

Immoral —not conforming or accepting standards of morality, *spiritual lostness.*

Immortal —*living forever, never dying or decaying for those in Jesus Christ.*

Impact —a substantial effect on others, highly influential, *make an impression for His glory.*

Impartial —treating everyone fairly and equally, *leaving all doors open as God does.*

Impatience —no patience, irritable, restless, *complete opposite of the Fruit of the Spirit.*

Imperative —necessary, mandatory, pressing, urgent, *could be dire — if not a Believer.*

Important —significant value, an effect on success, *like living out God's word daily.*

Impression —a feeling or opinion about someone, view, perception, the *image of Him in us.*

Impulsive —done without forethought, in many, if not all cases, *no spiritual discernment.*

Inclusive —*all around, all-embracing, and all in for the Lord —without hesitation.*

Indifference —lack of concern, interest, or sympathy, no feelings, *distant from Godliness.*

Incense *Spiritual* —are the things of worship that are *acceptably* perceived, such as confessions, adorations, and prayers — things from the thought and mouth that bear relation to the truths of faith.

Influencer —*the power and impact we have on others when God's word is thriving in us.*

Initiative —*ambition, motivation, and drive to assess God's word and move forward.*

Insecure —unstable, weak, *not firmly fixed or grounded in the blanket of God's security.*

Insensitive —showing no feelings for others, callous, *lacking God's guidance.*

Instructions —order, command, directive, requirement, *stipulations given in His word.*

Integrity —*Christlike quality of moral uprightness, high principles in line with God.*

Interests —wanting to learn more about something, attentive, *honest students of God's word.*

Intentional —done on purpose, deliberate, thought out, *knowingly pleasing Him daily.*

Intercessor —is someone who prays, petitions, or begs God in favor of another person. Jesus Christ is our Intercessor!

Interpret —explain the meaning of, *make clear, understand, and resolve for our good purpose.*

J

Jealousy —discontent, resentment, *it means we are not happy with what God's given us.*

Jesus Christ —*God incarnate, the second person of the Trinity, Lord, Redeemer, Messiah, King, Savior, Son of the Living God, Creator, Wonderful Counsellor, Righteous One, Bread of Life, Advocate, Lamb of God, Good Shepherd, Bridegroom, Son of Man, Alpha and Omega, The Way, Truth, and Life.*

Joined —fixed together, connected, attached, *yoked, chained, locked in with Him.*

Journey —the act of moving, *making one's way down God's path of Righteousness.*

Joy —*greatest of pleasures,* happiness, delight, *rejoicing, and exultation of our life in Christ.*

Judgment—Final —*unbelievers are judged for their sins and cast into eternal separation.* [insert sad face]

Judging —*determine the biblical act of righteous and unrighteous behavior in a believer.*

Justice —is rooted in the very nature of God as a Righteous Judge. He rewards good, and he does not ignore the sins of any; He renders to everyone what is due, which means we are held accountable.

Justified —*declared righteous because of our faith in what Christ did for us on the cross.*

K

Kindness —a *great concern for all, expecting nothing in return, genuine Godly sincerity.*

Knowing —realize, aware, understand, sense, recognize, *notice right from wrong.*

Knowledge —comprehend, mastered, accomplishment, intelligence, *God's insight.*

L

Lawlessness is the stage of a person's life where they are more defined by the acts of sin. It is contrary and opposite to God's way of living. It's the act of not regarding God's guidelines for holy living.

Learner —learning a subject or skill and utilizing *God's word in their life.*

Led —*to be prompted, instructed, and directed by the Holy Spirit—He leads our way.*

Legalism is a set of laws above the Gospel, emphasizing a system of rules and regulations for achieving salvation and spiritual growth, opposite *God's grace.*

Lessons —period of teaching, tutoring of the *Holy Spirit by God's word.*

Life —Living Intentionally For Eternity, *the culmination of our real life in Christ.*

Lifestyle —the way one lives, an *influenced behavior by the flesh or Spirit.*

Light —*the natural agent that stimulates light, brightness, the ray of Christ's Light in us.*

Lineage —ancestry, family, heritage, roots, background, bloodline, *succession.*

Listener —*an attentive, intentional person who listens, hears, and applies God's word.*

Living Out —*the strength of Christ's Spirit at work within us, illuminating His Joy.*

Love —undeniable longing for affection and *all-consuming passion of commitment to Christ.*

Lustful —overwhelming sinful desire, pleasing oneself, *no regard for consequences.*

Lying —untruthful, false, dishonest, deceptive, underhand, hollow-hearted, *spiritually ill.*

M

Magnify —*make something appear more prominent, maximize, amplify*, and *enhance His glory in you.*

Malicious —someone intending to harm; this *is evil intent — and not Christlike.*

Manage —*in charge of, control, take forward, and handle God's word in your daily life.*

Manipulate —control or influence someone unfairly, without scruples or *malicious maneuvering.*

Materialism —is a kind of worldliness where God is gradually pushed off into a small corner, and the *physical substance is more important than the spiritual matter.*

Maturity —developed, effective, and fruitful, *changed from pleasing self to pleasing God.*

Mindset —an established set of fixed and growing attitudes *based on what is going into the mind — could be the spiritual game—changer in our daily life.*

Mortal —a human being subject to death, *but if in Christ as their Savior, they are immortal.*

Mercy —pity, compassion, kindness, forgiveness, *withholding punishment deserved.*

Mercy Seat —the lid on top of the Ark of Covenant where God was supposed to be seated, and from this place, He would dispense mercy to man when the blood of the atonement was sprinkled there. Christ, Himself is designated as our "propitiation." All our sins are covered by means of His death and our response to Christ through our faith in Him. This ties together the Old and New Testament concepts regarding the covering of sin as exemplified by the mercy seat of God.

Mirror—*Spiritual* —*the transformed image of our new life — and look like Christ.*

Misled —*deceived by someone, led in the wrong direction, lacks wisdom.*

Motives —reason for doing something, not hidden, intention, motivation, *Godly purpose.*

Mourning —expressing deep sorrow for someone's death, grieving for, wailing, *temporary.*

N

Need —require something of a necessity, essential, *significant in our life, like Christ.*

Negative —no optimism, not desirable, pessimistic, bleak, harmful, *a spiritual detriment.*

Neglect —fail to care of properly, untended, abandoned, *forsake His righteous ways.*

Nurture —*care for — encourage the growth and development of the feeding of His word.*

O

Obedience —comply with an order, respectful, a duty, disciplined, *conforming to all His ways.*

Obligation —legally bound to perform a duty or personal responsibility; it is the *requirement to serve Him.*

Offering —voluntarily putting forward graciously; it is joyously *submitting a gift to Christ. It is our advancement to Him for His glory.*

Omnipotent —*unlimited power, able to do anything, Supreme, Most-High, invincible.*

Omnipresent —*present everywhere, infinite, boundless, immeasurable.*

Omniscient —*all-knowing, all-wise, and all-seeing.*

Opinion —a viewpoint or judgment formed about something, most notably those that *align with God's word.*

Opportunity —*chance, good time, occasion, moment, opening, option, go and seize — now.*

Opposition —one that opposes, combats, fights against, and antagonizes another for their belief in a cause, *such as the enemy and unbelieving world against Christians.*

Oppression —heavily weighed down in spirit, mind, or body, *but Jesus can set us free.*

Overcome —prevail, get the better of, beat, tame, subdue, *get over, solve, triumph over.*

P

Passover —commemorates the Hebrews' liberation from slavery in Egypt and the "passing over" of the forces of destruction and sparing of lives when the lamb's blood was marked on their doorposts. Christ can save us when we accept Him as Savior.

Past —gone by in time and no longer existing — *such as your sins when you accept Christ.*

Patience —*restraint, calm, tolerance, even temperedness, composed, kindness, tranquil.*

Peace —restful, free from disturbance, stillness, solitude, *lack of interruptions—rest in Him.*

Perception —ability to hear, see or be aware of something, *a notion of God's word.*

Perish —suffer death, expire, fall, *go the way of all flesh, be lost, eternal death.*

Persecution —hostility, ill-treatment, *unfairness, and cruelty over a prolonged period.*

Perseverance —determination, diligence, patience, resolve, steadfastness, and *commitment to Him.*

Perspective —view, outlook, position, interpretation, frame of mind, approach—*God's lens.*

Perpetual —never-ending, long-lasting, without end, but as *believers — permanently in Christ.*

Perversion is the distortion or alteration of someone living from the original design of God's creation. They are misrepresenting God's natural plan and into an absolute state of falsehood. This is not acceptable in the eyes of God.

Planning —*decide, arrange, organize, work out, and expect God's word to develop you.*

Plagues Spiritually —a contagious disease that causes distress, torture, and torment but can be *delivered and freed when we give our lives to Christ.*

Pleasing —feel happy, satisfied, pleasant, acceptable, enjoyable, and *delightful in Him.*

Pleasures —happiness, satisfaction, delight, gladness, contentment, *enjoy His provisions.*

Potential —*showing the capacity to develop into something, life in the making for God.*

Position —a situation, orientation, posture, attitude, *your place grounded in Him.*

Positive —optimism, confidence, *helpful, beneficial, cheerful, Godly encourager.*

Possession —*the ownership and control of God in us, proclaiming His excellencies.*

Power —*is an inherent characteristic of God, the Christian life is an empowerment from God, the same power that raised Christ from the dead indwells in believers today.*

Praise —*a wholehearted expression of approval, admiration, and commendation to Christ.*

Prayer —a precious avenue that God has provided where we can raise our hearts by talking to Him, communicating *all our thoughts, needs, and desires — it is an intentional act.*

Precept —*a principle or doctrine intended to regulate our behavior, such as God's word.*

Predestined —*it is the biblical doctrine that God, in all His sovereignty, chooses specific individuals to be saved, but the choice to accept Him is "always available for anyone."*

Preparation —devise, put together, get ready, train, educate, discipline, *Godly grooming.*

Prepare —*get into spiritual shape, equip oneself with the Armor of God, and put in action.*

Pressures —an unavoidable part of life on earth, a squeezing and crushing— is the application of any power, but as believers in Jesus Christ, He relieves us from these forces.

Pride —a sinful, arrogant, haughty, self-reliant attitude or spirit that causes a person to have an inflated or puffed—up view of themselves, *Kingdom Killer.*

Priests —A chosen leader who can draw near to God and minister. He alone is responsible for offering divinely appointed sacrifices to God, executing the different procedures and ceremonies relating to God's worship, and representing God and man. Still, today *our Mediator is Jesus Christ.*

Priority —*something significant that we care about, like our time in His Word*— regarded or treated as more important, first concern, *greatest importance.*

Procrastinate —*put off, delay, undecided, take one's time, tactic, hesitate, spiritually lazy.*

Produce —make, build, put together, assemble, process, *mass—produce for His glory.*

Progress —*moving forward, advancing, and making headway in our daily Christian life.*

Promise —One declaring they will do exactly what they say, *such as God's plans for our salvation and blessings to His people.*

Propitiation —appeasing the wrath of sinners—*reconciled to God because of Christ's sacrifice.*

Protector —One Who defends or shields from injury, evil, and oppression.

Provide —make available for use, supply, assign, present; He *bestowed for our service.*

Provider —God supplies the needs of all creation but gives special care to his own people.

Pruning —*cut away things in our spiritual life that are unproductive and hinder growth.*

Purging —*to purify and separate us from dirty things in our lives.*

Purify —cleanse, refine, freshen, *strain contaminants, sift, and make pure by God.*

Purpose —the reason something is done, *a Christlike desire to achieve a good and righteous outcome.*

Pursue —follow someone, go after, run after, chase, *proceed along His path constantly.*

Q

Quality —the degree of excellence, standard, condition, character, worth, and *Godly values.*

R

React —behave in a particular way, retaliate, oppose, revolt against, *conduct oneself.*

Reality —*the real world, the Godly truth of His existence at work in our real life.*

Rebellion —*an act of violent resistance, civil disobedience, disorder, unrest, or anarchy.*

Receptive —willing to consider and accept *the quality of receiving the Truth of His word.*

Recognize —*identity, acknowledge an area of concern, and gain support from the Lord.*

Redemption —the *act of being saved from sin; God paid it all through His Son—Jesus Christ.*

Reformed —*changed from worse to better — when we allow His Spirit to work in us.*

Refuge —a condition of being safe or sheltered from pursuit, haven: *He is our everyday security.*

Refuse —one who is unwilling to do something, rejected as worthless, *spiritual defeat.*

Rejection —refuse something that could be of benefit, *a danger to deny the truth of God.*

Rejoice —*feeling of unbelievable joy, transporting that delight back to the ears of God.*

Relationship —*connection, bond, relevance, association, be a part of God's family.*

Religion —*belief and worship of the One True God, genuine godliness in practice, performing all duties to God and our fellow believers, in obedience to His divine command.*

Remembrance —reminding ourselves of all God has done for us in Christ.

Remove —cut off, detach, *and separate ourselves from anything, not Christlike.*

Renewed —*a new person, restored life, spiritually new, a new creation in Christ as Lord.*

Repent —*change one's mind and attitude, purpose from a course of alarming conduct to God.*

Repetition —*repeating something, copying, quoting God's word daily.*

Representative —*characteristic illustrative, an exemplary of Christlikeness in our life.*

Reproach —*find unacceptable, object to, dislike, or be against, such as false teachings.*

Reprobate —an evildoer, wretched person, worthless, *and unacceptable to God.*

Reputation —a belief held about someone, overall quality recognized by others, *is the opinion of others, Christ, in you?*

Resolve —settle, find a solution to a problem, *sort out, clarify, and set right in His sight.*

Response —something said or done to react to something – *a productive answer.*

Responsibility —*Godly duty to deal with something that needs to be made right—lovingly.*

Rest —*a refreshed and recharged spirit when grounded and dependent upon the Lord.*

Results —the outcome, findings, effects, *the by-products of His fruits at work in our life.*

Resurrection —*a rising again— a return from death to life— as the resurrection of Christ, it is strength for today — and bright hope for tomorrow.*

Reunion —*a reuniting after separation, our glorious reconnection with fellow believers.*

Reverence —*high esteem, deep respect, our favor, worship, honor, and praise to God.*

Rewards —*Our Lord recompenses us out of His kindness in return for well— done services.*

Righteousness —morally correct, the highest honor, justifiable, rightness, *acceptable — Christ.*

Role —*our part and character on this earth that should display Christlike qualities.*

S

Safeguard —a measure taken to protect someone, a provision; our *buffer is Jesus Christ.*

Salvation —*being delivered, by God's grace, from sin and its consequence of eternal punishment and being raised to newness of life in Christ Jesus.*

Saved —*rescued and delivered* from the hands of the enemy and eternal death.

Sanctified —*to be set apart from the world and used for God's holy work.*

Satan —accuser, destroyer, deceiver, manipulator, liar, enemy, prince of evil spirits, *the adversary of God and Christ.*

Satisfied —meet the expectations, needs, or desires of pleased, *content with all of God.*

Sealed —*to guarantee security and indicate our authentic ownership of God in us.*

Seek —an attempt to find something, pursue it—chase after it, *a relentless quest for God.*

Self-Control —the *ability to control self in emotions, desires, words, and deeds, a Godly fruit.*

Selflessness —*more concerned with the needs and well—being of others than themselves.*

Selfishness —the excessive concern for oneself, *their advantage, and pleasure.*

Sensitivity —*aware of the needs and emotions of others, responds with Christlikeness.*

Sensuality —*enjoyment or pursuit of physical pleasure, a carnal passion of ungodliness.*

Servant —one who performs duties for others, *a selfless helper in all facets.*

Service —helping someone, *genuine Christlike kindness — keeps one in good condition.*

Shameful —causing disgrace, embarrassing, dishonorable, *Christ can remove all shame.*

Sharing —have a portion with another, participate in *our Christlike fellowship with others.*

Shrewd —clever, *calculating,* sharp-witted, canny, wise, *it is another enemy's mask.*

Sight —the ability to see, visual perception, observe and *make out the truth.*

Significant —*sufficiently of foremost importance, worthy of, notable* —like Christ in us.

Sin —wicked, morally wrong, fallen, unholy, tainted, impure, *failure to do what is right.*

Slander —a false statement damaging to a person; it is malicious lying, and *God hates it.*

Slave *Spiritual* —the "possession" of his master, in obedience to his commands, *their actions signify ownership* — *the flesh or the Spirit.*

Slow —*designed to do so unhurriedly, deliberately, unrushed, relaxed, comfortably, steadily, and quickly, a gentle approach in many cases spiritually driven.*

Sly —conniving, scheming, deceitful, *manipulative, sneaky, an enemy masquerade.*

Solidity —the quality of being firm or strong in structure, *your steadfastness in Christ.*

Sovereignty —*Supreme Authority, Power, Dominion, and Control.*

Speech —the ability to express inner thoughts; it *is the utterance of good or bad things.*

Spiritual —*living out God's presence in our life* — *in a way that glorifies Him.*

Spiritual *Leader* —a servant who *influences people to think, say and behave in ways that enhance their spiritual life to discipleship and service for the Lord.*

Standards —quality level, excellence worth, guideline, benchmark, *God's requirement.*

Steadfastness —*is your firm and unwavering faith in the Lord so that nothing can deter you.*

Steps —the act of movement, in stride, course of action, strategy, *an initiative to follow God.*

Steward —*a man's relationship to God, identifies God as owner — and man as a manager.*

Storm —*a rushing, raging, or violent agitation used to mature and strengthen* Christlikeness.

Strategy —an approach designed to achieve an overall aim, *a grand design of* Christlikeness.

Strengthen —become more assertive, to add, *increase* an obligation or authority.

Stronghold —*see Foothold.*

Stubborn —unwilling to change attitude or position, *inflexible, bull-headed, pigheaded.*

Stumbling Block —a thing or someone *who keeps another from a relationship with God.*

Submission —*obedient to Authority and the very act of submitting to them for control.*

Success —the outcome of an aim or purpose, *a victory when we yield to God's guidance.*

Suffering —hardship, distress, tribulation, pain, agony, sadness, *not for long as believers.*

Surrender —*choose to give up the fight between self and God and surrender to His will.*

T

Tabernacle —was the center of worship of Yahweh by the people of Israel shortly after the Exodus. It housed the ark of the covenant, representing God's presence and serving as a place of sacrifice and worship.

Talents —*gifts from God in the form of a person's calling or natural ability — glorify Him.*

Task —work *to be done, duty, responsibility, and charge—such as the Great Commission.*

Teaching —*is one of the gifts of the Holy Spirit, the ability to explain God's Word clearly, and instruct and communicate knowledge as it relates to the faith and truths of the Bible.*

Temptation —the desire or urge to do something *wrong or unwise.*

Ten Commandments —the moral law given to Moses provided the foundation for a new Israelite society. Jesus called people to an even higher standard by obeying the commandments not only in their actions but also in their hearts.

Tension —stress, anxiety, nervousness, agitation, pressure, *restlessness, uncertainty.*

Test —a *challenging situation that prompts us to discern how God would have us respond.*

Thankfulness —*should be a way of life, naturally flowing from our hearts and mouths every day - because God is worthy.*

Thoughts —*an idea produced by thinking of an image can be good or bad, depending on what we are feeding into our minds that can make something pure or impure.*

Time —an allotted or used moment that *can yield a negative or positive experience.*

Tithing —*a joyful, voluntary giver who trusts God* as the source of all He's given them to supply their needs — *they are a cheerful giver, giving back portions of God's blessings.*

Together —in alliance, bonded as one, cooperate, partners, *in one accord with God.*

Tolerance —allow and accept an occurrence or practice, *ensuring it aligns with Scripture.*

Tongue—*Spiritual —it is either honoring the Lord or spewing venom that God forbids.*

Transformed —changed, altered, reshaped, renewed, remade, *and made to be used.*

Transparent —see-through, uncloudy, clearly exposed, *real Christlikeness seen in you.*

Trial —a cause of great suffering, *cross to bear, but God will give us strength.*

Trust —*a bold, confident, sure of security; it is what we do because of the faith we're given; it is Godly trust that will not waiver because it is based on faith in the promises of God.*

Truth —the quality of our *factual, genuine, authentic, and valid position in Christ.*

Turn Away —move or face a different location, and *your shift from ungodliness to godliness.*

U

Unbeliever —someone who has rejected Jesus Christ and wants nothing to do with Him, but Christ wants something to do with you because He cares. [insert smiley face]

Unchanging —*someone not changing, staying the same, caught in the enemy's trap.*

Understanding —*perceive God's word with intended and accurate meaning so you can live a true intentional life for God today.*

Unforgiveness —a *solid unwillingness* to restore what is broken, like taking poison and expecting someone else to die, *a spiritual killer, He forgave — so we can forgive.*

Unholy —ungodly, godless, depraved, sinful, wicked *with no room in God's Kingdom.*

United —joined together for *a common purpose or familiar feeling with the Lord daily.*

Unity —joined as a whole, unified, *a oneness with God, identity, selfsameness.*

Unrest —*dissatisfaction, disturbed, and agitation when the Lord's absent.*

Urgent —immediate action, desperate, *a severe cry for God's help in a dire situation.*

Usefulness —*superior quality of having utilities —gifts —that bring value to God.*

Utilize —*make practical and effective use of, deploy, and bring into action for God.*

V

Valid —well-founded, sound, defendable, robust, dependable, *convincingly Christlike.*

Value —*level of something deserved, important, worthy, like our daily steps with God.*

Verify —*make sure, demonstrate, justify, authenticate, confirm,* and *substantiate Him in us.*

Victory —is *that place in our relationship with God because He gives us the advantage or power over spiritual enemies, temptations, or any struggle in life. In Christ, we have the ultimate victory and the power of His indwelling Spirit alive and at work in us daily.*

Violence —force intended to hurt, damage, or kill, cruel, brutal, *no spiritual control.*

Vital —necessary, essential, fundamental, needed, *highest priority, such as His word alive in us.*

W

Wait —*to stay for— rest or remain still in expectation of— wait for orders; it is the power of undeniable willingness and patience "in His strength" to get you to the next phase.*

Walking —*move regularly, accompany, guide, and move in stride with Christ daily.*

Want —a desire to possess, care for, crave, thirst for, desperate, *a yearning for Christ.*

Warning —*Caution against danger, faults, or evil practices that can lead us astray.*

Weakness —*means we do not have what it takes, and we desperately need God daily.*

Weariness —*the weight of the world and exhaustion of everyday life leads us to this overly debilitating state, so we need God as our focal point to help balance this life.*

Wealth —*Spiritual —God's intelligence and wisdom in our life and His knowledge of truth and good, but true wealth is eternal life in Christ.*

Wholly —*entirely all in without any reservation, and to the maximum extent for the Lord.*

Wilderness Spiritually —an uninhabited area where we spend time alone and encounter God. It has a purpose and plans in our life with meaning and real-life application.

Willing —ready, eager, prepared, intend, desire, order, command, *a want of Him in you.*

Wisdom —having experience, wise, knowledgeable, discerning, *Godly judgment.*

Witness —*someone who boldly and confidently conveys to the world the evidence of what Jesus Christ did to transform their life into a faithful and serving Believer.*

Worship —*that feeling of complete reverence and adoration for our Lord and King.*

Worry —*spiritual defeater that accomplishes nothing. However, Christians do not worry, for they trust God wholly.*

Worthy —*deserving merits, excellence in qualities, an important person like Christ.*

Y

Yearning —an intense longing for something, craving, hunger, the *eagerness of Him—now.*

Yielding —submissive, inclined to give in, compliant, *a person who is bendable to God.*

Yoke —*the weight of a task or obligation— if joined with the right and most effective partner, it goes in a direction that will yield a very productive Christlike result.*

Z

Zeal —incredible energy, enthusiasm, love, devotedness, appetite, vigor, and *a solid and undeniable passion for Him in my life today.*

Bibliography

American Center for Law and Justice. "Kids' Bibles Confiscated." *Archive of Political Emails*, January 31, 2023. https://politicalemails.org/messages/947656.

Caballes, Tom. "Pursuing Holiness in an Unholy World." *The Sword of the Spirit* (blog), April 1, 2019. https://swordofthespirit.net/pursuing-holiness/.

Emmons, Robert. "What Gets in the Way of Gratitude?" *Greater Goods Magazine*. November 12, 2013. https://greatergood.berkeley.edu/article/item/what_stops_gratitude.

Enduring Word Ministry. "Cleansing after Childbirth." https://enduringword.com/bible-commentary/leviticus-12.

———. "Gifts of the Twelve Tribes." https://enduringword.com/bible-commentary/leviticus-7.

———. "How to Co-Exist with a Holy God." https://overviewbible.com/leviticus.

———. "Instructions for the Priests." https://enduringword.com/bible-commentary/leviticus-6.

———. "Special Sabbaths and Jubilee." https://enduringword.com/bible-commentary/leviticus-25.

———. "The Conduct of Priests." https://enduringword.com/bible-commentary/leviticus-10.

———. "The Peace Offering." https://enduringword.com/bible-commentary/leviticus-3 Leviticus 3.

———. "The Sanctity of Blood." https://enduringword.com/bible-commentary/leviticus-17.

———. "The Trespass and Guilt Offering." David Gruzik on Spurgeon. https://enduringword.com/bible-commentary/leviticus-5.

Freedom Outpost. "Signs That America Has Become a Seriously Wicked Nation." *Investor Times*, June 11, 2015. https://investortimes.com/freedomoutpost/america-a-wicked-nation.

Got Questions. "Bible on Lawlessness." https://www.gotquestions.org/Bible-lawlessness.html.

———. "Do Christians Sin?" https://www.gotquestions.org/do-Christians-sin.html.

———. "How Can I Live a Holy Life?" https://www.gotquestions.org/holy-life.html.

———. "How Can I Tap into the Wisdom of God?" https://www.gotquestions.org/wisdom-of-God.html.

———. "Spiritual Discernment." https://www.gotquestions.org/spiritual-discernment.html.

————. "What Does the Bible Say About Tattoos?" https://www.gotquestions.org/tattoos-sin.html.

————. "What Is the Difference Between Righteousness and Holiness?" https://www.gotquestions.org/difference-righteousness-holiness.html.

————. "What Makes Sexual Sin Such a Big Deal." https://www.gotquestions.org/sexual-sin.html.

————. "What Is Spiritual Blindness." https://www.gotquestions.org/spiritual-blindness.html.

————. "Why Is Leprosy Talked about So Much in the Bible." https://www.gotquestions.org/Bible-leprosy.html.

————. "Without Holiness, No One Will See the Lord." https://www.gotquestions.org/without-holiness-no-one-will-see-the-Lord.html.

Hubbard, Scott. "How to Recognize the Holy Spirit." *Desiring God*, January 9, 2020. https://www.desiringgod.org/articles/how-to-recognize-the-holy-spirit.

Insight for Living Ministries Article (Canada). *The Bible Teaching Ministry of Charles R. Swindoll.* "John Wycliffe." May 27, 2022. https://www.insightforliving.ca/read/articles/john-wycliffe#.

Jones, Stephen. "Our Lifeline Is Christ (John 15:1–11)." *Sermons By Logos Site.* 2009. https://sermons.faithlife.com/sermons/85009-our-lifeline-is-christ.

Krantz, Jeffrey. "Leviticus: How to Coexist with an All-Powerful, Holy God." *Overview Bible*, July 1, 2013. https://overviewbible.com/leviticus/.

Navigators Site. "The Wheel Illustration." https://www.navigators.org/resource/the-wheel-illustration/.

North, Oliver, and David Goetsch. "Lawlessness in America: The 'Progressive' Culture of Death." *Townhill Column*, December 28, 2022. https://townhall.com/columnists/olivernorthanddavidgoetsch.

Barna Group. "The Concept of Holiness Baffles Most Americans." *The Christian Post*, February 21, 2006, https://www.christianpost.com/news/new-barna-survey-finds-most-americans-baffled-by-holiness.html.